WHIMSICAL WOODCRAFTS
TO MAKE & PAINT

WHIMSICAL
WOODCRAFTS
TO MAKE & PAINT

Patrick Lose

A Sterling / Chapelle Book
Sterling Publishing Co., Inc.   New York

Assistant to Patrick Lose: Lenny Houts

FOR CHAPELLE:

Owner:	Jo Packham
Editor:	Cathy Sexton
Staff:	Trice Boerens, Rebecca Christensen, Amber Fuller, Holly Fuller, Cherie Hanson, Holly Hollingsworth, Susan Jorgensen, Susan Laws, Amanda McPeck, Barbara Milburn, Jamie Pierce, Leslie Ridenour, Cindy Stoeckl, Nancy Whitley, and Lorrie Young
Photography:	Kevin Dilley for Hazen Photography
Technical Drawings:	Roxanne LeMoine
Woodworking Instructions:	Tony Lydgate

The author wishes to thank Chris Clark, for making many of the wood pieces in this book, and Beverly Rivers, for her technical advice, support, and, most of all, her friendship.

All original illustrations in this book are by Patrick Lose. If you would like more information about Patrick's designs and "Out on a Whim" patterns for wearable art, quilts, wood and holiday crafts, write to: Out on a Whim, P.O. Box 400, Van Meter, Iowa 50261.

For information on where to purchase kits or ready-to-paint pieces for the projects in this book, write to: Out on a Whim, P.O. Box 400, Van Meter, Iowa 50261.

Library of Congress Cataloging-in-Publication Data

Lose, Patrick.
    Whimsical woodcrafts to make & paint / Patrick Lose
            p.   cm.
    "A Sterling / Chapelle book."
    Includes index.
    ISBN 0-8069-1395-9
    1. Woodwork--Patterns.   2. Painted woodwork   3.Acrylic painting.
TT200.L67   1995
745.51--dc20

                                        95-11545
                                        CIP

10 9 8 7 6 5 4 3 2 1

Published by Sterling Publishing Company, Inc.
387 Park Avenue South, New York, NY 10016
© 1995 by Chapelle Ltd.
Distributed in Canada by Sterling Publishing
c/o Canadian Manda Group, One Atlantic Avenue, Suite 105
Toronto, Ontario, Canada M6K 3E7
Distributed in Great Britain and Europe by Cassell PLC
Wellington House, 125 Strand, London WC2R 0BB, England
Distributed in Australia by Capricorn Link (Australia) Pty Ltd.
P.O. Box 6651, Baulkham Hills, Business Centre, NSW 2153, Australia
Printed and Bound in Hong Kong
All Rights Reserved

Sterling ISBN-0-8069-1395-9

For Katie . . .
I love you.

— Dad

ABOUT THE AUTHOR

PATRICK LOSE has spent his professional years in a variety of creative fields. He began his career as a costume designer for stage and screen. Costume credits include more than 50 productions and work with celebrities such as Liza Minnelli and Jane Seymour.

An artist and illustrator since childhood, Patrick works in many mediums. When he sits down to "doodle" at the drawing board, he never knows what one of his designs might become. Whether it's a cross-stitch piece, wearable art, a greeting card, an ornament, or a piece of furniture, he enjoys creating it all.

His crafts, clothing, and home decorating accessories have appeared frequently in national magazines, including *Better Homes and Gardens, Country Crafts, Christmas Ideas, Halloween Tricks and Treats, Folk Art Christmas, Santa Claus, Decorative Woodcrafts, Craft and Wear,* and *American Patchwork and Quilting.* Publications featuring his designs have reached over 18 million subscribers.

OUT ON A WHIM, Patrick's company name, appropriately describes his original creations. Available in fabric and crafts stores nationwide, his patterns for making clothing, dolls, home decorating accessories, and holiday crafts feature folk-art whimsy with a contemporary twist.

CONTENTS

BEFORE YOU BEGIN

It's quite a challenge to combine a woodworking and a decorative painting book in one. I've tried to create projects to suit a variety of tastes and a variety of skill levels. Hopefully you'll find that this book offers something for everyone. As you read the instructions, you'll notice that we, the writers, have assumed that you will bring to each specific project the understanding and skill level necessary to complete construction and painting. If the project calls for the use of a band saw, for instance, we are assuming that you either know how to safely use one, or that you will enlist the assistance of someone who does. In any case, caution comes first when operating power tools and always wear safety glasses!

The patterns and painting techniques called for are based on simplicity. The lack of conformity in lines and shapes is part of the style of these pieces. You will find it much easier and more fun to draw a freehand line or shape than to use a straight edge to create it. My designs are a contemporary form of folk art with a "coloring book" style of painting. There is no "wrong" way to paint these pieces, so don't be intimidated. Simply use the instructions as a guide for your own creativity. If you feel that outlining and detailing is difficult with a round or liner brush, feel free to use a black Sharpie permanent marker, however, do not apply your finishing coat of acrylic spray after using the marker because it could smear or blur the lines.

I recommend that you use Baltic Birch plywood for the construction of the projects that call for plywood. Do not substitute a common construction-grade plywood, as Baltic Birch plywood is a sturdy wood that cuts, sands, and finishes like a nice piece of pine. It works wonderfully for thin and fragile project pieces. Baltic Birch plywood can be purchased through mail-order if you find it difficult to obtain at your lumber store.

There will be two names listed for each color in the materials list. The first will be the color name for the brand of acrylic paint that I chose to use for the projects in this book. In parenthesis will be a generic color name. If you choose to use the same brand of paint that I used, you can refer to page 142 for the color number. If you select another brand, use the name in parenthesis as a guide to selecting a color in that range. Be sure to experiment when mixing colors as directed in the text if you are using another brand. I can't guarantee that mixtures and ratios will remain the same. If the colors that have been used do not suit your taste, simply choose a different scheme of acrylic paints and create your own masterpiece! No matter how you choose to accomplish the projects, you'll be much happier with the results if you have fun in the process and my main purpose for writing this book is just that.

SHORT
ON TIME

Where does the time go?

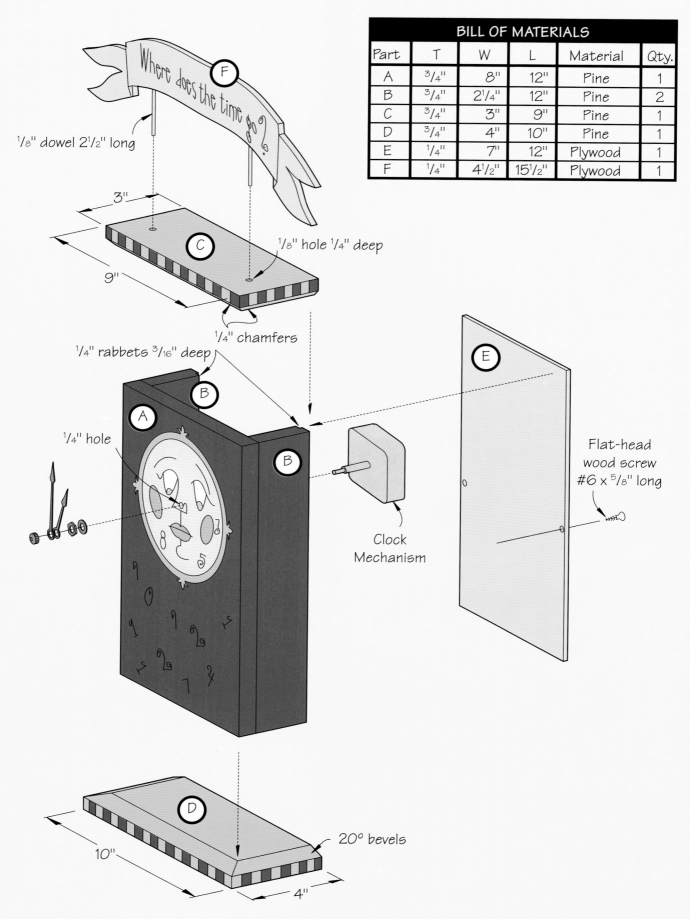

Where does the time go?

1/8" dowel 2 1/2" long

3"

9"

1/8" hole 1/4" deep

1/4" chamfers

1/4" rabbets 3/16" deep

1/4" hole

Clock Mechanism

Flat-head wood screw #6 x 5/8" long

20° bevels

10"

4"

12

SHORT ON TIME

WOODWORKING INSTRUCTIONS—

TOOLS & SUCH

Table saw
10" disc sander with
    adjustable table or
    6" x 48" belt sander
Band saw or scroll saw
Files
Drill
Drill bits
2 dowels, $1/8$" diameter, $2 1/2$" long
Sandpaper, medium-grit and
    fine-grit
Tack cloth
Wood glue
Clock mechanism,
    for a $3/4$"-thick clock face
2 flat-head wood screws,
    #6 x $5/8$" long
Screwdriver

CUT IT OUT

1 Except for the back (Part E) and the banner (Part F), all parts for this project are cut from $3/4$"-thick pine. After these parts have been cut on the table saw, add the chamfer on the top and the bevel on the bottom by using either a 10" disc sander with adjustable table or a 6" x 48" belt sander. (If these tools are not available, these details may be hand-carved or hand-planed). The banner is cut from $1/4$" plywood using a band or scroll saw, and the saw cuts are then cleaned up with files and hand sanding.

2 Drill holes in the banner as indicated on the pattern. Care must be exercised in drilling the holes to take the two dowels that attach it to the top. Since the thickness of the banner is $1/4$", and the diameter of the dowels is $1/8$", there is room for only $1/16$" of stock on either side of the dowel holes, so these must be exactly centered.

GET IT SANDED

1 Before assembly, make sure that all parts are finish sanded, with their sharp edges "killed" or slightly rounded, and that all tool marks are removed. Use a medium-grit sandpaper to sand the clock and banner. Switch to a fine-grit sandpaper and sand again. Then lightly wipe over all surfaces with a tack cloth to pick up the dust created by sanding. (Don't firmly rub the tack cloth over the wood—the cloth will leave an unwanted tacky residue.)

PUT IT TOGETHER

1 Run through a dry assembly first, without glue, to be sure all parts fit. Glue up the front, sides, bottom, and top. Once the glue has dried, you can begin painting. When painting is finished, install the clock mechanism, screw on the back, and add the banner.

SHORT ON TIME
PAINTING INSTRUCTIONS—

Pure Pigment Paint Colors
  Ivory Black
  Napthol Crimson
  Titanium White
Acrylic Paint Colors
  Almond Parfait (gray skintone)
  Berries 'n Cream (light mauve)
  Bluebell (medium aqua)
  Harvest Gold (deep gold)
  Heartland Blue (blue gray)
  Potpourri Rose (light mauve)
  School Bus Yellow (deep yellow)
  Taffy (off white)
Antiquing Medium
  Apple Butter Brown
Clear acrylic spray
Brown paper bag or old cotton rag
Tracing paper
#2 lead pencil
Graphite paper
White graphite paper
Paper towels
Round brush, #4 or #5
Flat brush
Liner brush
Stylus
Old toothbrush

1 Base-coat the clock face and sides Napthol Crimson and paint the top and base School Bus Yellow. Let the paint dry. Use a piece of brown paper bag or an old cotton rag to smooth the painted surfaces. Wipe off the sanding dust. (Acrylic paint often raises the grain of the wood.)

2 With tracing paper, duplicate the clock face pattern. Turn the tracing over and rub over the pattern lines with a #2 lead pencil. You may transfer the design with a commercial graphite paper, but you'll want to eliminate messy excess graphite by wiping over the graphite with a paper towel.

3 Transfer only the clock face rim onto the clock front. Base-coat the face Taffy and let the paint dry. Paint the checks on the top and on the base Napthol Crimson. (Don't attempt to make the checks perfectly matched in width. Part of the charm of folk art is the lack of conformity in shapes and style.) Outline the sides of each check with Ivory Black.

4 Paint the face rim School Bus Yellow and shade the rim with Harvest Gold. Use a round brush (a #4 or #5 works great) to add the Titanium White highlight lines.

5 Transfer the pattern details onto the face with white graphite paper. Paint the eyes Titanium White. Mix Heartland Blue and Bluebell, 2:1, and fill in the irises. Let the paint dry. Add Ivory Black pupils.

6 Mix Titanium White and Napthol Crimson, 5:1, and dip a large flat brush in the mixture. Then, wipe off most of the paint on a paper towel. Brush in the cheeks. Paint the lips with a mixture of equal parts of Berries 'n Cream and Potpourri Rose.

7 Using a liner brush, add the remaining clock face details and paint all of the numbers on the clock face and falling down the clock front Ivory Black. Dip the end of a stylus into Titanium White and dot the large pupil highlight. Without dipping the stylus back into the paint, dot the small iris highlight. Then, dip the stylus into the Titanium White and repeat the process for the opposite eye. Let the paint dry.

8 Paint the banner Taffy. Use a piece of brown paper bag or an old cotton rag to smooth the painted surfaces. Wipe off the sanding dust. Mix Taffy and Almond Parfait, 2:1, and shade the banner folds. Paint the letters and outline the banner shape with Ivory Black. Antique the banner and the dowels with Apple Butter Brown antiquing medium and let the antiquing dry. Thin the antiquing medium with water until it's the consistency of ink and, with an old toothbrush, flyspeck the clock front. To flyspeck, dip the bristles of the toothbrush into the thinned paint, then flick your thumb through the bristles to cause the paint to spatter off of the toothbrush. Flick first onto paper until your specks are the desired size and intensity, then flyspeck the clock front. Let the paint dry.

9 Apply clear acrylic spray to all wood surfaces. Finally, install the clock mechanism, screw on the back, and add the banner.

SHORT ON TIME

PATTERNS—

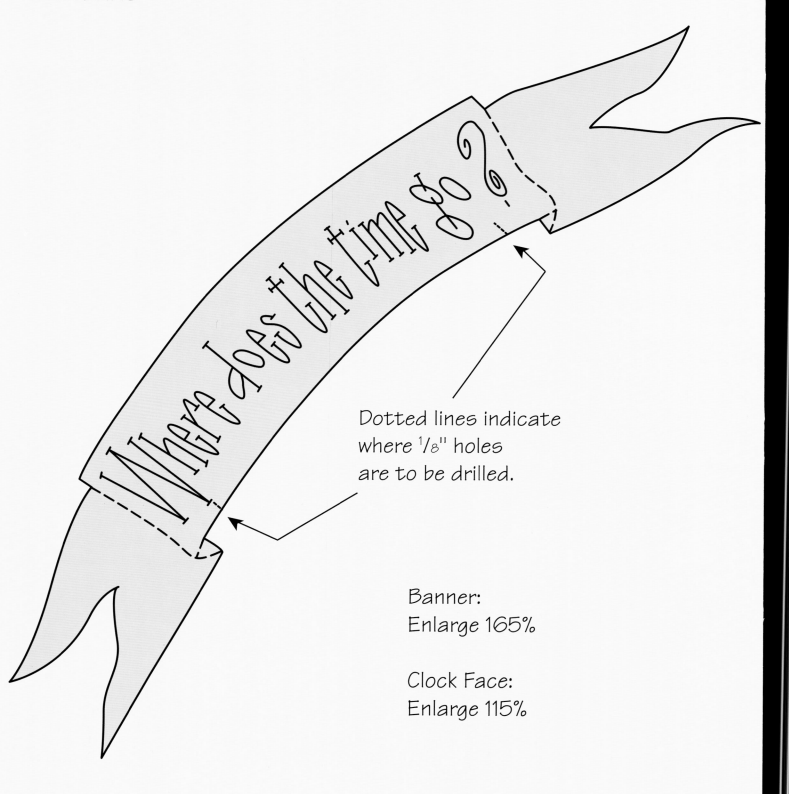

Dotted lines indicate
where 1/8" holes
are to be drilled.

Banner:
Enlarge 165%

Clock Face:
Enlarge 115%

SUN-KISSED
PAINTING INSTRUCTIONS—

DO IT LIKE THIS

1 Base-coat the inside and lip of the bowl Coastal Blue and paint the outside of the bowl Cobalt Blue. Let the paint dry. Use a piece of brown paper bag or an old cotton rag to smooth the painted surfaces. Wipe off the sanding dust. (Acrylic paint often raises the grain of the wood.)

2 With tracing paper, duplicate the sun pattern. Turn the tracing over and rub over the pattern lines with a #2 lead pencil. You may transfer the design with a commercial graphite paper, but you'll want to eliminate messy excess graphite by wiping over the graphite with a paper towel.

3 You'll find it almost impossible to lay the complete pattern inside the bowl to transfer the design, so we suggest you follow these steps. First, cut out the sun, carefully going around each ray point. Then, cut the center oval away from the rays, leaving you with two pieces—the oval face and the ray points. Position the center oval inside the bowl and draw around it with a #2 lead pencil. Then fit the rays around the oval, drawing around three or four rays at a time, before continuing around the oval.

4 Base-coat the sun face Yellow Medium. To fill in the rays, use a round brush (a #4 or #5 works great). Paint one ray at a time as follows: Fill in the first ray with Pure Orange. Before the paint dries, and without rinsing out the brush, pick up Yellow Medium and add a few strokes over the top of the orange. Do not overblend. Pick up Titanium White and apply a few

SUN-KISSED
PAINTING INSTRUCTIONS (CONTINUED)—

streaks over the first two colors. Continue around the oval until you complete all rays.

5 Dip a large flat brush in Pure Orange. Then, wipe off most of the paint on a paper towel. Add a light blush of cheek color to the sun face. Once all the paint dries, copy the features onto the face. Turn the face pattern over to the back side and rub over the pattern lines with a #2 lead pencil. Place the pattern on the base-coated face, graphite side down, and use a stylus or your pencil to transfer the details to the bowl.

6 Paint the eyes Titanium White. Fill in the irises with Coastal Blue. Let the paint dry. Add Ivory Black pupils. Using the round brush, outline the rays, face oval and eyes, and add the nose, mouth, and cheek spirals with Ivory Black. Dip the end of a stylus into Titanium White and dot the large pupil highlight. Without dipping the stylus back into the paint, dot the small iris highlight. Then, dip the stylus into the Titanium White and repeat the process for the opposite eye. Let the paint dry.

7 Now it's time to paint the clouds. If you've never tried painting clouds before, we suggest you get the feel by practicing on a piece of scrap paper or wood, as there is no pattern for the clouds. Paint about a third of the cloud border at one time. Wet the area by painting over it with the Coastal Blue base-coat color, using a flat brush that measures somewhere around 1" in width. Before the paint dries, pick up Titanium White on one brush corner and loosely "push" the color along the top of each cloud. As the Coastal Blue begins to dry, you may need to pick up a bit of the blue color on the flat brush, then dip the corner of the bristles back into the Titanium White. Let the paint dry.

8 Apply clear acrylic spray to the front, back, and lip of the bowl. If you plan to use the bowl for serving snacks, apply several coats of a good polyurethane finish. Once guests empty the bowl, wipe out the interior with a damp cloth. (Fruit and/or hot foods will damage the surface of the bowl.)

SUN-KISSED

PATTERN—

Sun:

Reproduce 100%

21

CRACKERS FOR KITTY

WOODWORKING INSTRUCTIONS—

TOOLS & SUCH

Pine, $\frac{1}{2}$" x 8" x 8"

Pine, 1" x 6" x 4"

Scroll saw

Tracing paper

#2 lead pencil

Graphite paper

Paper towels

Sandpaper, medium-grit and
    fine-grit

Tack cloth

Wood glue

Clamps

CUT IT OUT

1 With tracing paper, duplicate the patterns. Turn the tracing over and rub over the pattern lines with a #2 lead pencil. You may transfer the design with a commercial graphite paper, but you'll want to eliminate messy excess graphite by wiping over the graphite with a paper towel. Transfer the patterns onto the wood. Cut the cat face outline from $\frac{1}{2}$" pine. Cut the wood plug for the lid back from 1" pine.

GET IT SANDED

1 Before assembly, make sure that all parts are finish sanded, with their sharp edges "killed" or slightly rounded, and that all tool marks are removed. Use a medium-grit sandpaper to sand the saw-cut pieces. Switch to a fine-grit sandpaper and sand again. Then lightly wipe over all surfaces with a tack cloth to pick up the dust created by sanding. (Don't firmly rub the tack cloth over the wood—the cloth will leave an unwanted tacky residue.)

PUT IT TOGETHER

1 Center, glue, and clamp the wood plug to the back of the cat face cutout. Once the glue has dried, you can begin painting. When painting is finished, place the lid on the cookie jar. (If the cookie jar opening varies from the one used in this pattern, simply adjust the size of the wood plug.)

CRACKERS FOR KITTY

PAINTING INSTRUCTIONS—

STUFF YOU GOTTA HAVE

Glass cookie jar with
   3⅞" diameter opening
Pure Pigment Paint Colors
   Ivory Black
   Sap Green
Acrylic Paint Colors
   Georgia Peach (light skintone)
   Persimmon (rusty orange)
   School Bus Yellow (deep yellow)
   Strawberry Parfait (medium pink)
   Wicker White (white)
Clear acrylic spray
Black permanent marker
   with ultra-fine point
Brown paper bag or old cotton rag
#2 lead pencil
White graphite paper
Paper towels
Round brush, #4 or #5
Flat brush
Stylus

DO IT LIKE THIS

1 After you've prepared the wood, base-coat the entire cat lid Georgia Peach. Let the paint dry. Use a piece of brown paper bag or an old cotton rag to smooth the painted surfaces. Wipe off the sanding dust. (Acrylic paint often raises the grain of the wood.)

2 Transfer the cat face onto the lid with white graphite paper. Mix Persimmon and Georgia Peach, 2:1, and paint the hair tuft and the spots. While the paint is still wet, pull streaks (cat hairs) of Persimmon, then Georgia Peach, through the areas in a direction to simulate hair growth. Blend slightly.

3 Mix equal parts of Strawberry Parfait and Wicker White and paint the nose. Reapply Georgia Peach to the inside of the ears. Before the color dries, brush in a small amount of the mixture made for the nose. Fill in the eye areas with Wicker White. Mix equal parts of Sap Green and School Bus Yellow and paint the irises. Fill in the pupils, add the top eyelid, and paint the mouth and the line around the nose with Ivory Black. Dip the end of a stylus into Wicker White and dot the large pupil highlight. Without dipping the stylus back into the paint, dot the small iris highlight. Then, dip the stylus into the Wicker White and repeat the process for the opposite eye. Let the paint dry.

4 Apply clear acrylic spray to all wood surfaces. Using the black marker, outline the eyes and irises, the nose, the inner ears, the hair tuft and the spots, and add the whiskers. Do not apply any finish once you've added the black details. Finally, place the lid on the cookie jar.

CRACKERS FOR KITTY

PATTERNS—

Cat Face:
Enlarge 125%

Wood Plug:
Enlarge 125%

SPICE UP
YOUR LIFE

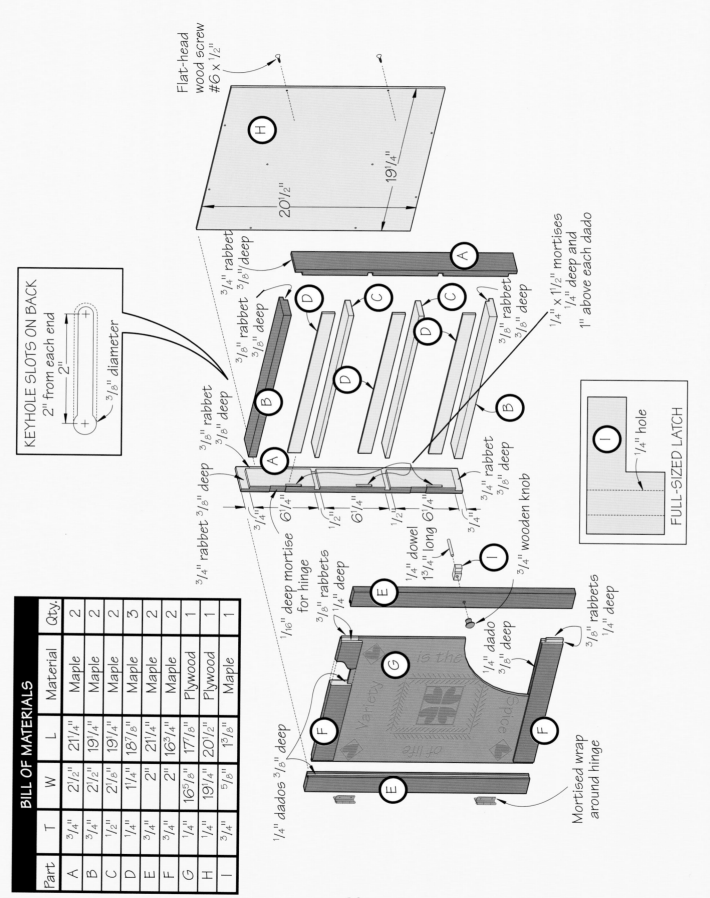

BILL OF MATERIALS

Part	T	W	L	Material	Qty.
A	3/4"	2 1/2"	21 1/4"	Maple	2
B	3/4"	2 1/2"	19 1/4"	Maple	2
C	1/2"	2 1/8"	19 1/4"	Maple	2
D	1/4"	1 1/4"	18 7/8"	Maple	3
E	3/4"	2"	21 1/4"	Maple	2
F	3/4"	2"	16 3/4"	Maple	2
G	1/4"	16 5/8"	17 7/8"	Plywood	1
H	1/4"	19 1/4"	20 1/2"	Plywood	1
I	3/4"	5/8"	1 3/8"	Maple	1

Flat-head wood screw #6 x 1/2"

KEYHOLE SLOTS ON BACK
2" from each end
2"
3/8" diameter

3/4" rabbet 3/8" deep
3/8" rabbet 3/8" deep
3/8" rabbet 3/8" deep
3/8" rabbet 3/8" deep
3/4" rabbet 3/8" deep
3/4" rabbet 3/8" deep
3/4" rabbet 3/8" deep

1/4" x 1 1/2" mortises 1/4" deep and 1" above each dado

1/16" deep mortise for hinge
3/4" 6 1/4" 1/2" 6 1/4" 1/2" 6 1/4" 3/4"

1/4" dowel 13 1/4" long
3/4" wooden knob

1/4" hole
FULL-SIZED LATCH

3/8" rabbets 1/4" deep
3/8" rabbets 1/4" deep
1/4" dado 3/8" deep
1/4" dados 3/8" deep

Variety is the Spice of life

Mortised wrap around hinge

28

SPICE UP YOUR LIFE

WOODWORKING INSTRUCTIONS—

TOOLS & SUCH

Table saw

Plane

Chisel

Sandpaper, medium-grit and
    fine-grit

Tack cloth

Wood glue

2 hinges

8 flat-head wood screws,
    #6 x $\frac{1}{2}$" long

Screwdriver

Dowel, $\frac{1}{4}$" diameter, $1\frac{3}{4}$" long

Wooden knob, $\frac{3}{4}$"

CUT IT OUT

1 Start by making the sides (Part A), the bottom and top (Part B), and the shelves and guard rails (Parts C and D), all of which are similar in shape and dimension. Using $\frac{3}{4}$"-thick maple, rough-cut the shelves and guard rails, then plane the shelves down to $\frac{1}{2}$" thickness, and the guard rails down to $\frac{1}{4}$". After planing, trim these and all parts to required final dimensions. Two pieces of $\frac{1}{4}$" maple veneer plywood are used for the cabinet back (Part H) and the door panel (Part G).

2 Cut the required dados and rabbets using the table saw. The hinge mortises on the left side (Part A) may be cut by hand using a sharp chisel. Since it is both difficult and dangerous to cut small parts on the table saw, special care must be taken in making the latch (Part I). The best way is to rip a rabbet in a $1\frac{3}{8}$"-wide length of $\frac{3}{4}$"-thick maple that is not shorter than 10", then crosscut to produce the $\frac{5}{8}$"-long latch.

GET IT SANDED

1 Before assembly, make sure that all parts are finish sanded, with their sharp edges "killed" or slightly rounded, and that all tool marks are removed. Use a medium-grit sandpaper to sand the cabinet. Switch to a fine-grit sandpaper and sand again. Then lightly wipe over all surfaces with a tack cloth to pick up the dust created by sanding. (Don't firmly rub the tack cloth over the wood—the cloth will leave an unwanted tacky residue.)

PUT IT TOGETHER

1 Run through a dry assembly first, without glue, to be sure all parts fit. Glue up the door, then glue up the body of the cabinet, with sides, top and bottom, and back. Finally, add the guard rails. Once the glue has dried, you can begin painting. When painting is finished, add the hinges, attach the door and the latch, and install the wooden knob.

SPICE UP YOUR LIFE
PAINTING INSTRUCTIONS—

STUFF YOU GOTTA HAVE

Acrylic Paint Colors
    Barnyard Red (rusty red)
    Harvest Gold (deep gold)
    Old Ivy (deep green)
Clear acrylic spray
Wood sealer
Masking tape
Brown paper bag or old cotton rag
Tracing paper
#2 lead pencil
Graphite paper
White graphite paper
Paper towels
Round brush, #4 or #5
Flat brush
Liner brush

DO IT LIKE THIS

1 Mask off the edge of the cabinet interior with masking tape. Seal the inside of the cabinet with wood sealer according to manufacturer's instructions. Let the sealer dry. Use a piece of brown paper bag or an old cotton rag to smooth the sealed surfaces. Wipe off the sanding dust. (Sealer often raises the grain of the wood.) Remove the masking tape.

2 Base-coat the edge and outside of the cabinet with Barnyard Red. Paint the frame of the door Barnyard Red and the door insert panel Harvest Gold. Repeat the colors on the inside of the door and panel. Paint the door hardware Harvest Gold. Let the paint dry. Use a piece of brown paper bag or an old cotton rag to smooth the painted surfaces. Wipe off the sanding dust. (Acrylic paint often raises the grain of the wood.)

3 With tracing paper, duplicate the pattern. Turn the tracing over and rub over the pattern lines with a #2 lead pencil. You may transfer the design with a commercial graphite paper, but you'll want to eliminate messy excess graphite by wiping over the graphite with a paper towel.

4 Transfer the design onto the cabinet insert panel with white graphite paper. Paint the center and corner squares, the lettering, and the "feather stitching" Old Ivy. Add Barnyard Red hearts and dots. Let the paint dry.

5 Apply clear acrylic spray to the interior and the exterior of the cabinet. Finally, add the hinges, attach the door and the latch, and install the wooden knob.

SPICE UP YOUR LIFE

PATTERNS—

Design:
Enlarge 180%

Variety is the spice of life

Lettering:
Enlarge 180%

COME ON IN

PATTERNS—

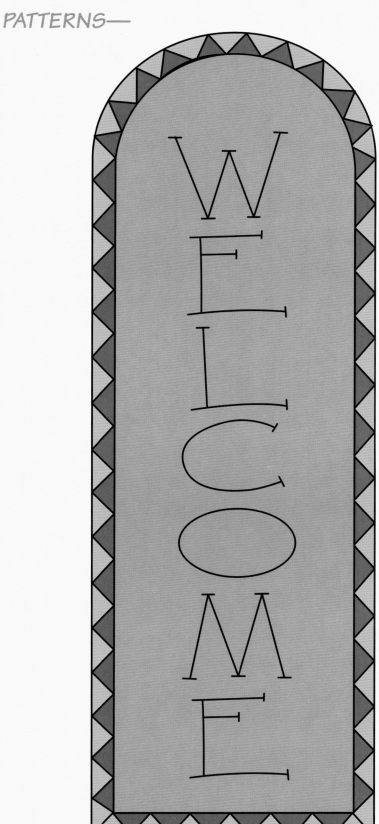

Welcome Sign:
Enlarge 205%

Heart:
Enlarge 205%

COME ON IN
WOODWORKING INSTRUCTIONS—

TOOLS & SUCH

Pine, $\frac{1}{2}$" x $18\frac{1}{2}$" x $6\frac{1}{2}$"
Plywood, $\frac{1}{4}$" x $7\frac{1}{2}$" x 12"
Scroll saw
Tracing paper
#2 lead pencil
Graphite paper
Paper towels
Drill
Drill bit, $\frac{1}{16}$"
Sandpaper, medium-grit and fine-grit
Tack cloth
16-gauge wire
Broom handle
5-minute epoxy
Sawtooth picture hanger

CUT IT OUT

1 With tracing paper, duplicate the patterns. Turn the tracing over and rub over the pattern lines with a #2 lead pencil. You may transfer the design with a commercial graphite paper, but you'll want to eliminate messy excess graphite by wiping over the graphite with a paper towel. Transfer the patterns onto the wood. Cut the sign board from $\frac{1}{2}$" pine. Cut three hearts from $\frac{1}{4}$" plywood. Drill $\frac{1}{16}$" holes in the sign board edges and in the heart edges to join the two. Do not join the pieces until you've finished the painting.

GET IT SANDED

1 Before assembly, make sure that all parts are finish sanded, with their sharp edges "killed" or slightly rounded, and that all tool marks are removed. Use a medium-grit sandpaper to sand the sign board and hearts. Switch to a fine-grit sandpaper and sand again. Then lightly wipe over all surfaces with a tack cloth to pick up the dust created by sanding. (Don't firmly rub the tack cloth over the wood—the cloth will leave an unwanted tacky residue.)

PUT IT TOGETHER

1 You can now begin painting. When painting is finished, install the sawtooth picture hanger at the center top of the back of the sign board.

2 Wrap 8" lengths of 16-gauge wire around a broom handle to coil. Pull the coils off the handle and use 5-minute epoxy to attach a heart to one end of each wire coil. Then, epoxy the opposite ends into the holes in the sides of the sign board. Let the epoxy set and twist the hearts into desired position.

COME ON IN
PAINTING INSTRUCTIONS—

STUFF YOU GOTTA HAVE

Pure Pigment Paint Colors
  Burnt Sienna
  Ivory Black
  Napthol Crimson
  Pure Orange
Acrylic Paint Colors
  School Bus Yellow (deep yellow)
Antiquing Medium
  Apple Butter Brown
Clear acrylic spray
Brown paper bag or old cotton rag
Ruler
#2 lead pencil
White graphite paper
Paper towels
Round brush, #4 or #5
Flat brush
Stylus
Woodburner, optional
Brass plumber's brush, optional
Tack cloth, optional
Old toothbrush

DO IT LIKE THIS

1 After you've prepared the wood, measure in $5/8"$-$3/4"$ from the outer edges of the sign board front and draw a pencil line. Use your pencil to draw the triangles along the border. Make certain you have enough triangles to alternate colors completely around the board. (Don't attempt to make the triangles perfectly matched in shape. Part of the charm of folk art is the lack of conformity in shapes and style.)

2 Use a woodburner to burn all penciled border lines. Continue the pattern on the sides of the board. If you've never used a woodburner, here are some important things to remember: Set the tip down and pull it toward you, following the pattern lines. For even lines, keep the tool moving at an even pace. To remove carbon buildup on the tip, use a brass plumber's brush. Use tack cloth to wipe away the woodburned particles.

If you prefer, paint the triangles without burning the lines.

3 Paint all Pure Orange triangles and let the paint dry. Then paint the Napthol Crimson triangles. Next, paint the board edges Pure Orange. Fill in the board front with School Bus Yellow and paint the three hearts Napthol Crimson. Let the front dry thoroughly; then immediately turn the board over and paint the board back Pure Orange. With a narrow board of this length, if you leave the back unpainted, you invite board warpage. The moisture content in the piece of wood you purchase may vary greatly from one lumber company to the next. Sealing only one surface with paint means that the untreated side continues to dry out and shrink, thus causing the board to bend in shape. Let the back dry thoroughly. Use a piece of brown paper bag or an old cotton rag to smooth the painted surfaces. Wipe off the sanding dust. (Acrylic paint often raises the grain of the wood.)

4 Transfer the lettering onto the sign board with white graphite paper. Paint the lettering Ivory Black. Let the paint dry. Dip the small end of a stylus into Napthol Crimson and apply small dots evenly along the lines. Let the dots dry thoroughly.

5 Antique all board surfaces with Apple Butter Brown antiquing medium and let the antiquing dry. Thin Burnt Sienna with water until it's the consistency of ink and, with an old toothbrush, flyspeck the sign board. To flyspeck, dip the bristles of the toothbrush into the thinned paint, then flick your thumb through the bristles to cause the paint to spatter off of the toothbrush. Flick first onto paper until your specks are the desired size and intensity, then flyspeck the sign board. Let the paint dry.

6 Apply clear acrylic spray to all wood surfaces. Finally, install the sawtooth picture hanger and attach the hearts, twisting them into desired position.

EASTER PARADE

PAINTING INSTRUCTIONS—

Small wooden box with handle
Pure Pigment Paint Colors
   Dioxazine Purple
   Phthalo Green
   Red Light
   Titanium White
Acrylic Paint Colors
   Green (medium green)
   Magenta (bright pink)
   School Bus Yellow (deep yellow)
   Sweetheart Pink (pink)
Clear acrylic spray
Black permanent marker
   with ultra-fine point
Brown paper bag or old cotton rag
Tracing paper
#2 lead pencil
Graphite paper
White graphite paper
Paper towels
Round brush, #4 or #5
Flat brush
Liner brush

DO IT LIKE THIS

1 Base-coat the entire wooden box, inside and out, including the handle, with Phthalo Green. Let the paint dry. Use a piece of brown paper bag or an old cotton rag to smooth the painted surfaces. Wipe off the sanding dust. (Acrylic paint often raises the grain of the wood.)

2 With tracing paper, duplicate the pattern. Turn the tracing over and rub over the pattern lines with a #2 lead pencil. You may transfer the design with a commercial graphite paper, but you'll want to eliminate messy excess graphite by wiping over the graphite with a paper towel.

3 Transfer the bunnies onto each end of the wooden box with white graphite paper. Next, transfer the eggs onto both sides of the wooden box with white graphite paper.

4 Base-coat both bunnies and all the eggs Titanium White. If necessary, apply a second coat of Titanium White to the bunnies. Transfer the pattern details with graphite paper. Paint the details on the bunnies and on the eggs with the remaining colors of paint.

5 Apply clear acrylic spray to all wood surfaces. Using the black marker, outline the bunnies and the eggs and add all remaining details. Do not apply any finish once you've added the black details.

EASTER PARADE
PATTERNS—

Rabbit:
Reproduce 100%

Eggs:
Reproduce 100%

HOME
TWEET
HOME

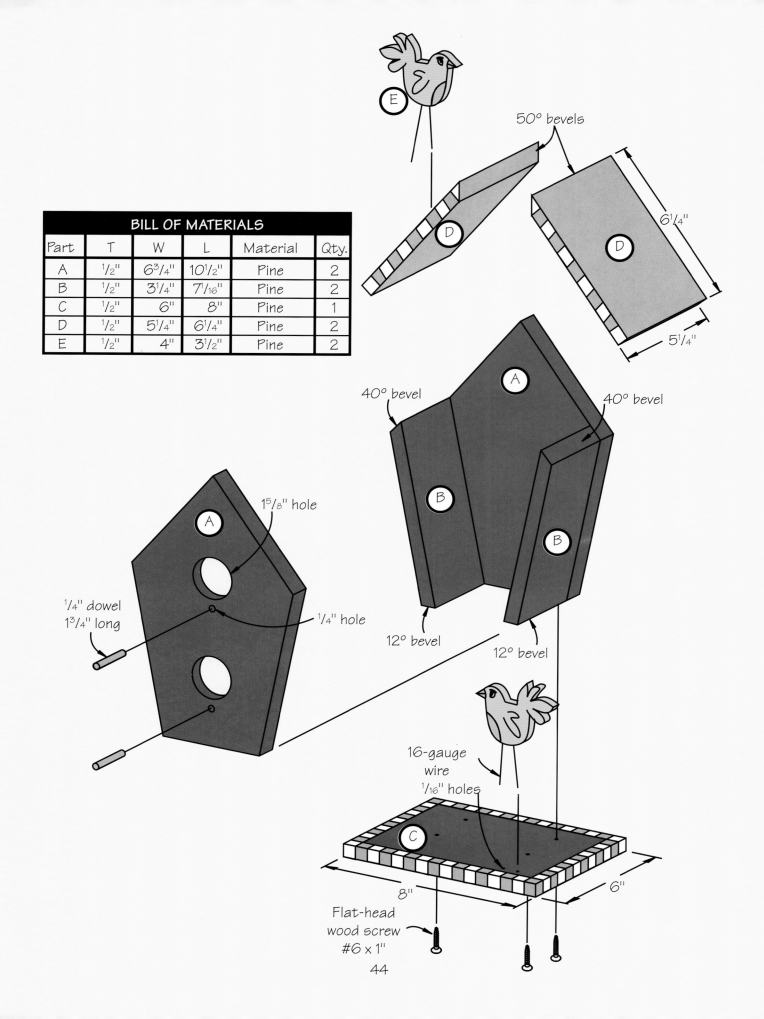

BILL OF MATERIALS

Part	T	W	L	Material	Qty.
A	$1/2$"	$6^3/4$"	$10^1/2$"	Pine	2
B	$1/2$"	$3^1/4$"	$7^1/{16}$"	Pine	2
C	$1/2$"	6"	8"	Pine	1
D	$1/2$"	$5^1/4$"	$6^1/4$"	Pine	2
E	$1/2$"	4"	$3^1/2$"	Pine	2

E

50° bevels

D

D

$6^1/4$"

$5^1/4$"

40° bevel

A

40° bevel

B

B

$1^5/8$" hole

A

$1/4$" dowel
$1^3/4$" long

$1/4$" hole

12° bevel

12° bevel

16-gauge
wire

$1/{16}$" holes

C

8"

6"

Flat-head
wood screw
#6 x 1"

HOME TWEET HOME
WOODWORKING INSTRUCTIONS—

TOOLS & SUCH

Table saw
6" x 48" belt sander
Band saw or scroll saw
Drill
Drill bits
Drill press or saber saw
Sandpaper, medium-grit and
   fine-grit
Tack cloth
2 dowels, $1/4$" diameter, $1^3/4$" long
Wood glue
12 flat-head wood screws,
   #6 x 1" long
Screwdriver
16-gauge wire

CUT IT OUT

1 All the parts for this project are made of $1/2$"-thick pine. Make the two roof pieces (Part D) from a pine board $5^1/4$"-wide by about 13" long, cross-cutting into two pieces each with a finished length of $6^1/4$". Do the same for the two sides (Part B). To cut the bevels, set the table saw blade at the appropriate angle, then crosscut. In making parts which have an angle at either end, be especially careful before you make your cuts: it's easy to get them backwards. The simplest way to make the pentagonal shape of the front/back (Part A) is to mark out the shape on a pine board using the template provided, then stack the two pieces together and carefully band or scroll saw.

2 Drill the holes for the perch dowels and the wood screws that hold the birdhouse to the base. The entry holes can be cut with a $1^5/8$"-diameter hole saw-mounted on a drill press, or by hand with a saber saw.

3 For the birds, plane pine to $1/2$" thickness. Draw an appropriate template, and cut the birds on the band saw, preferably stacked and clamped so that you make both at once, thereby ensuring they are identical in size and shape.

GET IT SANDED

1 Before assembly, make sure that all parts are finish sanded, with their sharp edges "killed" or slightly rounded, and that all tool marks are removed. Use a medium-grit sandpaper to sand the saw-cut pieces. Switch to a fine-grit sandpaper and sand again. Then lightly wipe over all surfaces with a tack cloth to pick up the dust created by sanding. (Don't firmly rub the tack cloth over the wood—the cloth will leave an unwanted tacky residue.)

HOME TWEET HOME
WOODWORKING INSTRUCTIONS (CONTINUED)—

PUT IT TOGETHER

1 Run through a dry assembly first, without glue, to be sure all parts fit. Lay the back down flat on the workbench and glue the sides in place. Apply glue to the end-grain edges, then put on the front. Finally, add the top and base. Once the glue has dried, any rough edges can be sanded smooth on the 6" x 48" belt sander. You can now begin painting. When painting is finished, cut three 1½" lengths and one 2" length of 16-gauge wire. Install the legs in the birds, the dowels in the birdhouse, and the birds on the birdhouse roof and base.

PATTERN—

Bird:
Reproduce 100%

HOME TWEET HOME

PAINTING INSTRUCTIONS—

STUFF YOU GOTTA HAVE

Pure Pigment Paint Colors
  Ivory Black
  Napthol Crimson
  Pure Orange
  Titanium White
Acrylic Paint Colors
  School Bus Yellow (deep yellow)
Antiquing Medium
  Apple Butter Brown
Clear acrylic spray
Black permanent marker
  with medium point
Brown paper bag or old cotton rag
Ruler
Tracing paper
#2 lead pencil
Graphite paper
White graphite paper
Paper towels
Round brush, #4 or #5
Flat brush
Stylus
Woodburner, optional
Brass plumber's brush, optional
Tack cloth, optional

DO IT LIKE THIS

1 After you've prepared the wood, measure in $5/8$" from the outer edges of the base and draw a pencil line. Use your pencil to draw the checks along the border. Make certain you have enough checks to alternate colors completely around the base. (Don't attempt to make the checks perfectly matched in width. Part of the charm of folk art is the lack of conformity in shapes and style.)

2 Use a woodburner to burn all penciled border lines. Continue the pattern on the sides of the base. If you've never used a woodburner, here are some important things to remember: Set the tip down and pull it toward you, following the pattern lines. For even lines, keep the tool moving at an even pace. To remove carbon buildup on the tip, use a brass plumber's brush. Use tack cloth to wipe away the woodburned particles.

If you prefer, paint the checks without burning the lines.

HOME TWEET HOME

DO IT LIKE THIS (CONTINUED)

3 Paint all Ivory Black checks on the base and on the roof and let the paint dry. Thin the Titanium White with water until it's the consistency of ink and paint the Titanium White checks. This allows the wood grain to show through. Next, paint the sides of the birdhouse and the area inside the base checks Napthol Crimson. Base-coat the area inside the checks on the roof Ivory Black. Paint the dowels Ivory Black. Let the paint dry. Use a piece of brown paper bag or an old cotton rag to smooth the painted surfaces. Wipe off the sanding dust. (Acrylic paint often raises the grain of the wood.)

4 With tracing paper, duplicate the bird pattern. Turn the tracing over and rub over the pattern lines with a #2 lead pencil. You may transfer the design with a commercial graphite paper, but you'll want to eliminate messy excess graphite by wiping over the graphite with a paper towel.

5 Transfer the bird pattern and base-coat the birds School Bus Yellow. Paint the wings Pure Orange. Fill in the eyes with Titanium White. Let the paint dry. Use a piece of brown paper bag or an old cotton rag to smooth the painted surfaces. Wipe off the sanding dust.

6 Transfer the details onto the birds with white graphite paper. Using the black marker, add the details on the birds. Dip the end of a stylus into Titanium White and dot the large pupil highlight. Antique all painted surfaces with Apple Butter Brown antiquing medium and let the antiquing dry.

7 Apply clear acrylic spray to all wood surfaces. Finally, install the legs in the birds, the dowels in the birdhouse, and the birds on the birdhouse roof and base.

HOME TWEET HOME
PATTERN—

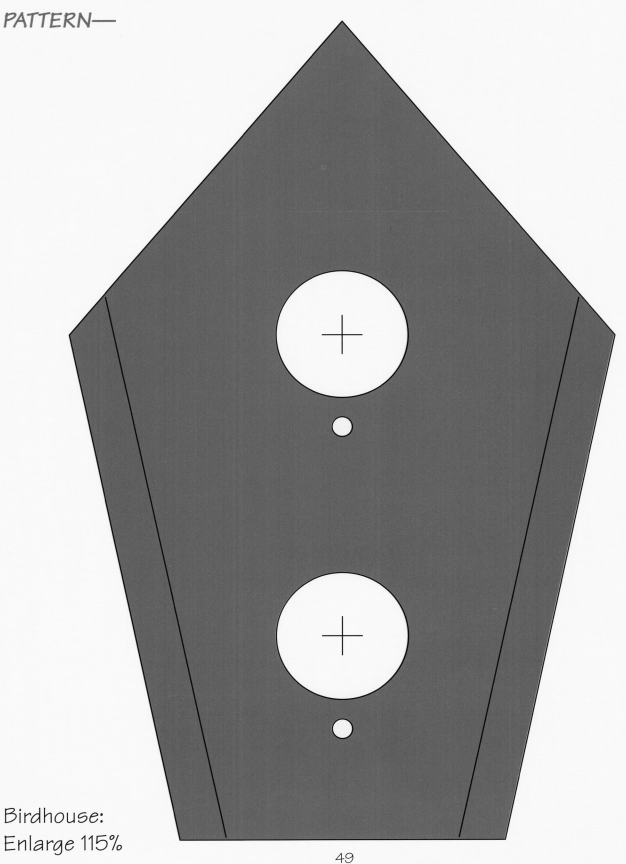

Birdhouse:
Enlarge 115%

49

MERRY
MEALS

BILL OF MATERIALS

Part	T	W	L	Material	Qty.
A	$1/2$"	$4^1/2$"	$13^3/4$"	Pine	2
B	$1/2$"	$4^1/2$"	$5^3/4$"	Pine	2
C	$1/2$"	$7^5/8$"	$14^3/4$"	Pine	2
D	$1/4$"	$4^1/2$"	6"	Plywood	1

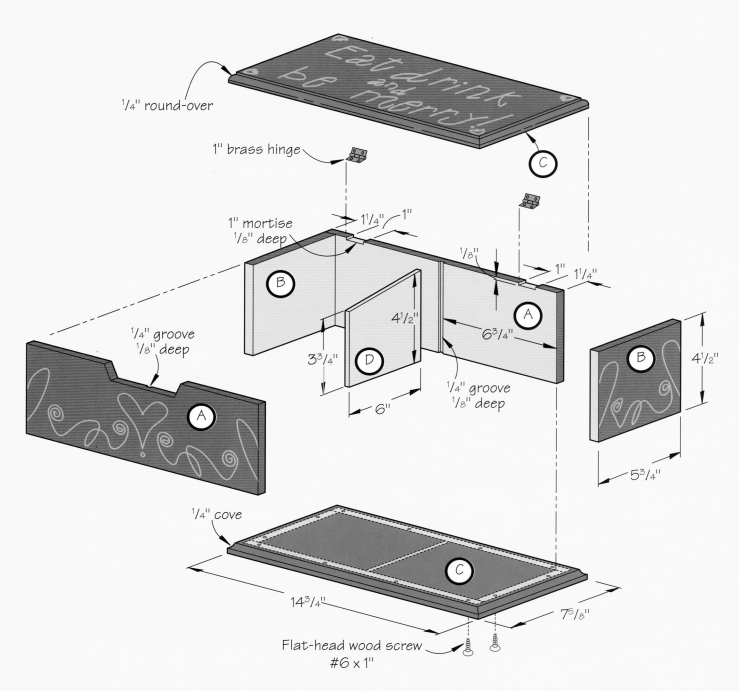

$1/4$" round-over

"Eat drink and be merry!"

1" brass hinge

1" mortise
$1/8$" deep

$1^1/4$" 1"

$1/8$" 1" $1^1/4$"

B

$1/8$"

A

$1/4$" groove
$1/8$" deep

$4^1/2$"

$3^3/4$"

D

6"

$6^3/4$"

$1/4$" groove
$1/8$" deep

B

$4^1/2$"

$5^3/4$"

A

$1/4$" cove

C

$14^3/4$"

$7^5/8$"

Flat-head wood screw
#6 x 1"

MERRY MEALS
WOODWORKING INSTRUCTIONS—

CUT IT OUT

1 All the parts for this project are made of ½"-thick pine, with the exception of Part D, the divider, which is made of ¼" plywood. The edges of the top and bottom are cut on a shaper using the appropriate round-over and cove bits. The groove on the insides of the front and back (Part A) is made on the table saw using either the dado blade or two passes with a regular table saw blade. The hinge mortises in the back can be cut by hand using a sharp chisel. Mill the thumb opening in the front using a band saw, then finish the cut with files and hand sanding.

GET IT SANDED

1 Before assembly, make sure that all parts are finish sanded, with their sharp edges "killed" or slightly rounded, and that all tool marks are removed. Use a medium-grit sandpaper to sand the recipe box. Switch to a fine-grit sandpaper and sand again. Then lightly wipe over all surfaces with a tack cloth to pick up the dust created by sanding. (Don't firmly rub the tack cloth over the wood—the cloth will leave an unwanted tacky residue.)

PUT IT TOGETHER

1 This box is put together using simple unreinforced butt joints, with the bottom screwed on. Run through a dry assembly first, without glue, to be sure all parts fit. Glue up the body of the box first, making sure it is exactly square. Once the glue has dried, carefully screw the bottom to this assembly and drop in the divider. You can now begin painting. When painting is finished, add the hinges and attach the lid.

MERRY MEALS

PAINTING INSTRUCTIONS—

STUFF YOU GOTTA HAVE

Acrylic Paint Colors
  Buttercrunch (light beige)
  Old Ivy (deep green)
  Sunset Orange (burnt orange)
Water-base stain,
  light pine or oak
Clear acrylic spray
Brown paper bag or old cotton rag
Tracing paper
#2 lead pencil
Graphite paper
Paper towels
Round brush, #3, #4, or #5
Flat brush
Stylus

DO IT LIKE THIS

1 Paint the sides and lid top Sunset Orange. Paint the routered base, the bottom of the chest, the routered lid edges, and the underside of the lid Old Ivy. Let the paint dry. Use a piece of brown paper bag or an old cotton rag to smooth the painted surfaces. Wipe off the sanding dust. (Acrylic paint often raises the grain of the wood.)

2 With tracing paper, duplicate the patterns. Turn the tracing over and rub over the pattern lines with a #2 lead pencil. You may transfer the design with a commercial graphite paper, but you'll want to eliminate messy excess graphite by wiping over the graphite with a paper towel.

3 Transfer the designs onto the box using the side and front patterns. Thin Buttercrunch with water until it's the consistency of ink. Using a round brush (a #3, #4, or #5 works great), paint the details. Dip the end of a stylus into Buttercrunch and add the heart dots.

4 Stain the inside of the box with a light pine or oak stain. Let the stain dry thoroughly. Apply clear acrylic spray to all wood surfaces. Finally, add the hinges and attach the lid.

MERRY MEALS

PATTERNS—

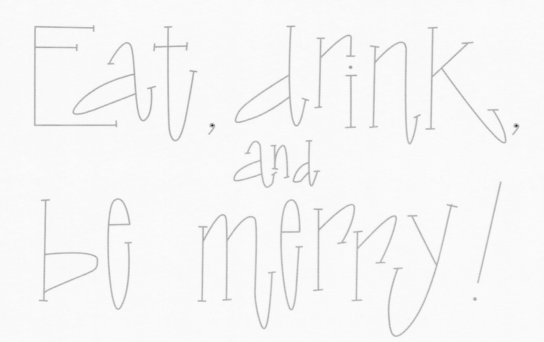

Design for Sides

Lettering & Hearts:
Enlarge 185%

Designs:
Enlarge 175%

Front Design

PICTURE PERFECT
WOODWORKING INSTRUCTIONS—

TOOLS & SUCH

Plywood, $3/8$" x $11^1/2$" x 10"
Plywood, $1/8$" x $7^1/4$" x $9^1/4$"
Scroll saw
Drill
Drill bit, $1/8$"
Tracing paper
#2 lead pencil
Graphite paper
Paper towels
Sandpaper, medium-grit and
   fine-grit
Tack cloth
3 brass screws, $3/8$" long
Screwdriver
Sawtooth picture hanger

CUT IT OUT

1 With tracing paper, duplicate the pattern. Turn the tracing over and rub over the pattern lines with a #2 lead pencil. You may transfer the design with a commercial graphite paper, but you'll want to eliminate messy excess graphite by wiping over the graphite with a paper towel. Transfer the pattern, including the interior and exterior cuts, onto the plywood. Drill $1/4$" start holes in the frame opening and the areas between the ribbon and frame. Make the interior cuts first. Then, cut the picture frame from $3/8$" plywood. Cut the frame back from $1/8$" plywood.

GET IT SANDED

1 Before assembly, make sure that all parts are finish sanded, with their sharp edges "killed" or slightly rounded, and that all tool marks are removed. Use a medium-grit sandpaper to sand the frame and frame back. Switch to a fine-grit sandpaper and sand again. Then lightly wipe over all surfaces with a tack cloth to pick up the dust created by sanding. (Don't firmly rub the tack cloth over the wood—the cloth will leave an unwanted tacky residue.)

PUT IT TOGETHER

1 You can now begin painting. When painting is finished, install the sawtooth picture hanger at the center top of the frame back. Position the back over the back of the frame and drill the $1/8$" pilot holes. Then, attach the back to the frame with $3/8$" brass screws. Tighten the screws after you've inserted your photograph. Do not put a screw at the top—leave it open for the photograph. Finally, insert your favorite photograph and tighten the brass screws.

PICTURE PERFECT

PAINTING INSTRUCTIONS—

STUFF YOU GOTTA HAVE

Pure Pigment Paint Colors
  Burnt Sienna
  Cerulean Blue Hue
  Ivory Black
  Napthol Crimson
Acrylic Paint Colors
  School Bus Yellow (deep yellow)
Clear acrylic spray
Gold marker
  with extra-fine point
Brown paper bag or old cotton rag
Paper towels
Round brush, #4 or #5
Flat brush
Liner brush

DO IT LIKE THIS

1 After you've prepared the plywood, base-coat the ribbon Napthol Crimson and the frame School Bus Yellow. Let the paint dry. Use a piece of brown paper bag or an old cotton rag to smooth the painted surfaces. Wipe off the sanding dust. (Acrylic paint often raises the grain of the wood.)

2 Add Ivory Black stripes to the ribbon and Cerulean Blue Hue dots to the frame. (Don't attempt to make the ribbon stripes perfectly matched in width. Part of the charm of folk art is the lack of conformity in shapes and style.) Make large and small dots on the frame. Let the paint dry.

3 Thin Burnt Sienna with water to create a stain and wipe over the frame surfaces to antique the paint. Let the antiquing dry. (If you prefer, you may use your favorite antiquing medium.)

4 Apply clear acrylic spray to all wood surfaces. Using the gold marker, outline the ribbon, the stripes, and the circles. Do not apply any finish once you've added the gold details. Finally, install the sawtooth picture hanger, attach the frame back to the frame with brass screws, insert your favorite photograph, and tighten the brass screws.

PICTURE PERFECT

PATTERN—

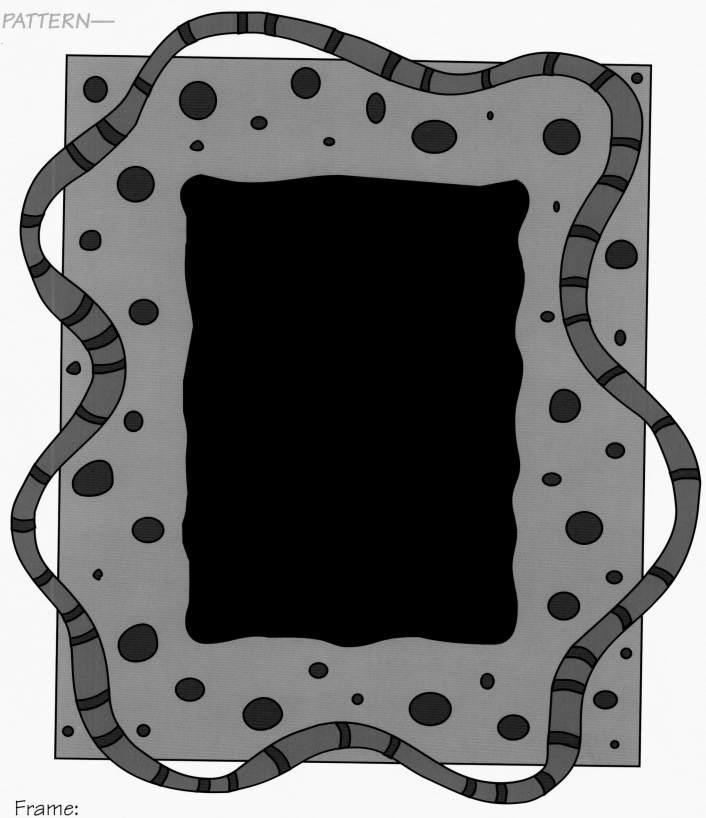

Frame:
Enlarge 120%

ANGELIC REFLECTIONS
WOODWORKING INSTRUCTIONS—

TOOLS & SUCH

2 pine boards, $^3/_4$" x $2^1/_2$" x 20"
2 pine boards, $^3/_4$" x $2^1/_2$" x 18"
Plywood, $^1/_4$" x $6^1/_4$" x $13^1/_4$"
Mirror, $^1/_4$" x $13^1/_2$" x $15^1/_2$"
Scroll saw
Tracing paper
#2 lead pencil
Graphite paper
Paper towels
Sandpaper, medium-grit and
    fine-grit
Tack cloth
Wood glue
2 sawtooth picture hangers

CUT IT OUT

1 Cut the frame from the 3/4"-thick pine. Cut the ends of the boards on an angle.

2 With tracing paper, duplicate the pattern. Turn the tracing over and rub over the pattern lines with a #2 lead pencil. You may transfer the design with a commercial graphite paper, but you'll want to eliminate messy excess graphite by wiping over the graphite with a paper towel. Transfer the pattern onto the plywood. Cut the angel cutout from the $^1/_4$" plywood.

GET IT SANDED

1 Before assembly, make sure that all parts are finish sanded, with their sharp edges "killed" or slightly rounded, and that all tool marks are removed. Use a medium-grit sandpaper to sand frame and angel cutout. Switch to a fine-grit sandpaper and sand again. Then lightly wipe over all surfaces with a tack cloth to pick up the dust created by sanding. (Don't firmly rub the tack cloth over the wood—the cloth will leave an unwanted tacky residue.)

PUT IT TOGETHER

1 Construct the frame from the $^3/_4$" thick pine. Miter the corners and put the four frame pieces together. Do not place the mirror into the frame until the frame has been painted.

2 You can now begin painting. When painting is finished, glue the angel cutout onto the mirror frame. Install the sawtooth picture hangers on the top of the back of the frame—one on the left, and one on the right.

ANGELIC REFLECTIONS

PAINTING INSTRUCTIONS—

STUFF YOU GOTTA HAVE

Pure Pigment Paint Colors
Ivory Black
Acrylic Paint Colors
Barnyard Red (rusty red)
Christmas Red (bright red)
Country Twill (beige)
Georgia Peach (light skintone)
Persimmon (rusty orange)
Primrose (salmon)
School Bus Yellow (deep yellow)
Shamrock (medium green)
Taffy (off white)
Wicker White (white)
Antiquing Medium
Apple Butter Brown
Clear acrylic spray
Brown paper bag or old cotton rag
#2 lead pencil
White graphite paper
Paper towels
Round brush, #4 or #5
Flat brush
Liner brush
Wood glue
Clamps

DO IT LIKE THIS

1 Base-coat the frame Shamrock. If necessary, apply another coat of Shamrock. Let the second coat dry. Base-coat the angel cutout Wicker White. Let the paint dry. Use a piece of brown paper bag or an old cotton rag to smooth the painted surfaces. Wipe off the sanding dust. (Acrylic paint often raises the grain of the wood.)

2 Transfer the hearts onto the frame with white graphite paper. Transfer the pattern details onto the angel cutout with white graphite paper.

3 Mix Christmas Red and Primrose, 2:1, and fill in the hearts on the frame. Outline the hearts with Ivory Black.

4 Using the Christmas Red and Primrose mixture, paint the heart on the angel cutout. Mix School Bus Yellow and Persimmon, 3:1, and paint the halos. Paint the angels' hands, feet, and face Georgia Peach. Paint their hair Barnyard Red and their robes Country Twill, using Shamrock for the hem trim. Paint the wings Taffy. Do the outlining and detail painting with Ivory Black, including the dots on the clouds.

5 Antique all surfaces with Apple Butter Brown antiquing medium and let the antiquing dry.

6 With wood glue and clamps (be careful not to scratch the paint), attach the angel cutout to the mirror frame. Let the glue dry and remove the clamps.

ANGELIC REFLECTIONS

PATTERNS—

Angels:
Enlarge 135%

Heart:
Reproduce 100%

SCHOOL DAYS
WOODWORKING INSTRUCTIONS—

TOOLS & SUCH

Plywood, 12" x 14"
Scroll saw
Tracing paper
#2 lead pencil
Graphite paper
Paper towels
Sandpaper, medium-grit and
   fine-grit
Tack cloth
5 button covers

CUT IT OUT

1 With tracing paper, duplicate the patterns. Turn the tracing over and rub over the pattern lines with a #2 lead pencil. You may transfer the designs with a commercial graphite paper, but you'll want to eliminate messy excess graphite by wiping over the graphite with a paper towel. Transfer the patterns onto the plywood. Using a scroll saw, cut out all five button cover shapes.

GET IT SANDED

1 Before assembly, make sure that all parts are finish sanded, with their sharp edges "killed" or slightly rounded, and that all tool marks are removed. Use a medium-grit sandpaper to sand the saw-cut pieces. Switch to a fine-grit sandpaper and sand again. Then lightly wipe over all surfaces with a tack cloth to pick up the dust created by sanding. (Don't firmly rub the tack cloth over the wood—the cloth will leave an unwanted tacky residue.)

PUT IT TOGETHER

1 You can now begin painting. When painting is finished, glue the painted pieces onto button covers.

SCHOOL DAYS
PAINTING INSTRUCTIONS—

STUFF YOU GOTTA HAVE

Pure Pigment Paint Colors
  Ivory Black
  Napthol Crimson
  Titanium White
Acrylic Paint Colors
  Berries 'n Cream (light mauve)
  Buckskin Brown (medium brown)
  Cotton Candy (light pink)
  Dove Gray (light gray)
  Earthenware (rusty brown)
  Evergreen (medium green)
  School Bus Yellow (deep yellow)
  Ultramarine (dark blue)
  Victorian Rose (light skintone)
Clear acrylic spray
Black permanent marker
  with ultra-fine point
Brown paper bag or old cotton rag
Tracing paper
#2 lead pencil
Graphite paper
White graphite paper
Paper towels
Round brush, #4 or #5
Flat brushes

DO IT LIKE THIS

1 Paint the frame on the blackboard Earthenware. Paint the blackboard Ivory Black. Let the paint dry. Transfer the lettering onto the blackboard with white graphite paper. Thin Titanium White with a little water to make it appear transparent, and paint the lettering. Apply clear acrylic spray. Using the black marker, add the wood grain detail to the blackboard frame.

2 Paint the apple Napthol Crimson. Use Titanium White for highlights on the apple. Paint the stem Earthenware and the leaf Evergreen. Apply clear acrylic spray. Using the black marker, outline the apple and add the veins in the leaf.

3 Paint the faces on the boy and the girl Victorian Rose. Paint the hair on the boy Buckskin Brown and the hair on the girl with a 3:1 mixture of School Bus Yellow and Titanium White. Paint the bow in the girl's hair Ultramarine. With a 1:1 mixture of Napthol Crimson and Titanium White, add the "blush" at the end of the smiles on both faces. The freckles on the boy's face are small dots of watered-down Earthenware. Apply clear acrylic spray. Using the black marker, add all outlining and face details.

4 Paint the pencil eraser Berries 'n Cream. Paint the eraser crimp Dove Gray. Paint the pencil School Bus Yellow. Paint the exposed wood on the pencil Cotton Candy. Paint the pencil lead Ivory Black with Titanium White highlights. Apply clear acrylic spray. Using the black marker, add all outlining.

SCHOOL DAYS

PATTERNS—

Button Cover Shapes:
Reproduce 100%

COUNTIN'
SHEEP

THE BRIDGES OF MADISON COUNTY   WALLER

HOW TO MAKE AN AMERICAN QUILT   WHITNEY OTTO

Sweet • *Dreams*

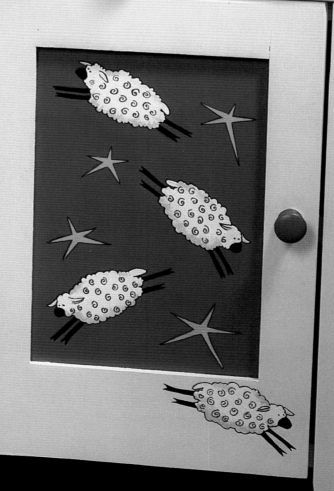

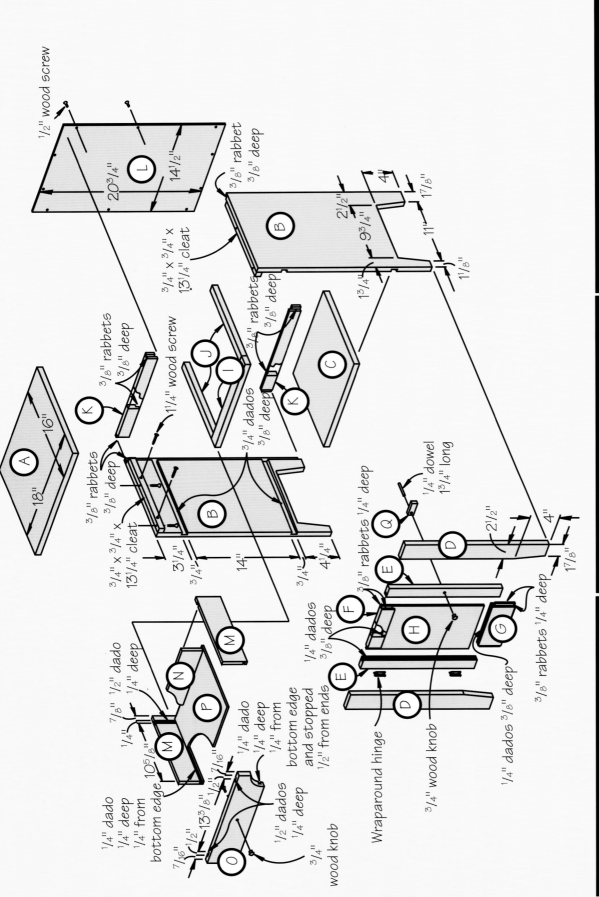

1/2" wood screw

20 3/4"

14 1/2"

3/8" rabbet
3/8" deep

L

3/4" x 3/4" x
13 1/4" cleat

B

2 1/2"

9 3/4"

4"

17/8"

11"

1 1/8"

13/4"

3/8" rabbets
3/8" deep

3/4" rabbets
3/8" deep

J

I

K

1 1/4" wood screw

C

3/8" rabbets
3/8" deep

16"

A

18"

3/8" rabbets
3/8" deep

3/4" x 3/4" x
13 1/4" cleat

B

3 1/4"

14"

3/4"

4 1/4"

3/4"

1/4" dowel
13/4" long

Q

3/8" rabbets 1/4" deep

E

D

2 1/2"

4"

17/8"

1/4" dados
3/8" deep

F

E

H

3/4" wood knob

D

G

3/8" rabbets 1/4" deep

1/4" dados 3/8" deep

Wraparound hinge

1/4" dado
1/4" deep
1/4" from
bottom edge

7/8"

1/4"

1/2" dado
1/4" deep

N

M

P

M

10 5/8"

13 3/8"

1/2"

7/16"

1/4" dado
1/4" deep
1/4" from
bottom edge
and stopped
1/2" from ends

1/2" dados
1/4" deep

3/4"
wood knob

O

7/16"

1/2"

BILL OF MATERIALS

Part	T	W	L	Material	Qty.
A	3/4"	16"	18"	Maple	1
B	3/4"	14"	23"	Maple	2
C	3/4"	13 5/8"	14 1/2"	Maple	1
D	3/4"	2 1/2"	19"	Maple	2
E	3/4"	1 1/2"	15"	Maple	2
F	3/4"	1 3/4"	7 1/2"	Maple	1

BILL OF MATERIALS

Part	T	W	L	Material	Qty.
G	3/4"	3"	7 1/2"	Maple	1
H	1/4"	7 5/8"	12 1/8"	Plywood	1
I	3/4"	15/8"	14 1/2"	Maple	1
J	3/4"	1"	13 5/8"	Maple	2
K	3/4"	1 1/2"	14 1/2"	Maple	2
L	1/4"	14 1/2"	20 3/4"	Plywood	1

BILL OF MATERIALS

Part	T	W	L	Material	Qty.
M	1/2"	3 1/4"	12"	Maple	2
N	1/2"	2 3/4"	13 1/8"	Maple	1
O	3/4"	3 7/8"	15 1/4"	Maple	1
P	1/4"	11 3/8"	13 1/8"	Maple	1
Q	1/2"	3/4"	2"	Maple	1
Cleat	3/4"	3/4"	13 1/4"	Pine	2

COUNTIN' SHEEP
WOODWORKING INSTRUCTIONS—

TOOLS & SUCH

Table saw
4 two-by-four blocks
Newspaper
Scraper
Abrasive planer or
   4" x 24" belt sander
Band saw
Files
Drill
Drill bits
Sandpaper, medium-grit and
   fine-grit
Tack cloth
Wood glue
2 wraparound hinges
10 flat-head wood screws,
   #6 x $1/2$" long
8 flat-head wood screws,
   #8 x $1^1/4$" long
Screwdriver
Dowel, $1/4$" diameter, $1^3/4$" long
2 wooden knobs, $3/4$"

CUT IT OUT

1 Start by making the panels that will become the top (Part A), the sides (Part B), and the bottom (Part C). Each of these parts will be made by edge gluing two or more boards to produce the desired width. The bottom can be made of $3/4$" maple veneer plywood; simply apply iron-on maple wood tape to the front edge.

2 Part A, the top, for example, needs a finished width of 16". Depending on the stock available to you, you might edge-glue three $5^1/2$"-wide boards, four 4" boards, or some other combination. Make sure the edges are as straight as your tools will permit, by joining them or ripping with great care on the table saw. Be careful that the clamping force is not so great that it causes the panel to curve or scoop across its width; a good way to prevent this is to "sandwich-clamp" either end of the panel between a pair of two-by-four blocks, each about as long as the panel is wide. Use a single thickness of newspaper to keep from gluing the two-by-fours to the panel (or the panel to your workbench!).

COUNTIN' SHEEP
WOODWORKING INSTRUCTIONS (CONTINUED)—

CUT IT OUT (CONTINUED)

3 Once these panels are complete, remove the excess glue with a scraper, and sand both faces flat using an abrasive planer, a 4" x 24" belt sander, or hand tools. Trim to dimension. On each of the two sides (Part B), cut out the space between the feet using a band saw, as well as the flare on the bottom sections of the front legs (Part D). The saw cuts are then cleaned up with files and hand sanding.

4 The rabbets and dados are cut using a dado blade on the table-saw. (Maple is a hardwood, so best results will be achieved by using carbide-tipped blades throughout.) Cut and install the cleats on the sides. Make sure the holes going through these cleats, which will eventually hold the screws fastening the top, are properly sized to allow the screws to pass through, and set far enough out (or slightly angled) so that you can get your hand and a screwdriver in to attach them.

GET IT SANDED

1 Before assembly, make sure that all parts are finish sanded, with their sharp edges "killed" or slightly rounded, and that all tool marks are removed. Use a medium-grit sandpaper to sand the night stand. Switch to a fine-grit sandpaper and sand again. Then lightly wipe over all surfaces with a tack cloth to pick up the dust created by sanding. (Don't firmly rub the tack cloth over the wood—the cloth will leave an unwanted tacky residue.)

PUT IT TOGETHER

1 Run through a dry assembly first, without glue, to be sure all parts fit. Glue up the door and the drawer, making sure both are square. Glue up the carcase with back. Once the glue has dried, you can begin painting. When painting is finished, install the wooden knobs and add the hinges. Attach the door, the latch, and the top.

COUNTIN' SHEEP
PAINTING INSTRUCTIONS—

DO IT LIKE THIS

1 Mask off the edge of the night stand interior with masking tape. Seal the inside of the night stand with wood sealer according to manufacturer's instructions. Let the sealer dry. Use a piece of brown paper bag or an old cotton rag to smooth the sealed surfaces. Wipe off the sanding dust. (Sealer often raises the grain of the wood.) Remove the masking tape.

2 Base-coat the edge and outside of the night stand Taffy. Paint the frame of the door Taffy and the door insert panel Blue Ribbon. Repeat the colors on the inside of the door and panel. Paint the knobs Blue Ribbon. Let the paint dry. Use a piece of brown paper bag or an old cotton rag to smooth the painted surfaces. Wipe off the sanding dust. (Acrylic paint often raises the grain of the wood.)

3 With tracing paper, duplicate the patterns. Turn the tracing over and rub over the pattern lines with a #2 lead pencil. You may transfer the design with a commercial graphite paper, but you'll want to eliminate messy excess graphite by wiping over the graphite with a paper towel.

4 Transfer the designs onto the night stand insert panel, the drawer, and the door frame with white graphite paper. Paint the lettering Blue Ribbon. Base-coat the sheep Titanium White. Paint the stars School Bus Yellow. Paint the legs Ivory Black. Fill in the ears with Cotton Candy. Let the paint dry. Using Ivory Black, outline the sheep and the stars, and add all details to the sheep.

5 Apply clear acrylic spray to the interior and the exterior of the night stand. Finally, install the wooden knobs and add the hinges. Attach the door, the latch, and the top.

COUNTIN' SHEEP
PATTERNS—

Lettering:
Reproduce 100%

Sheep & Stars:
Enlarge 110%

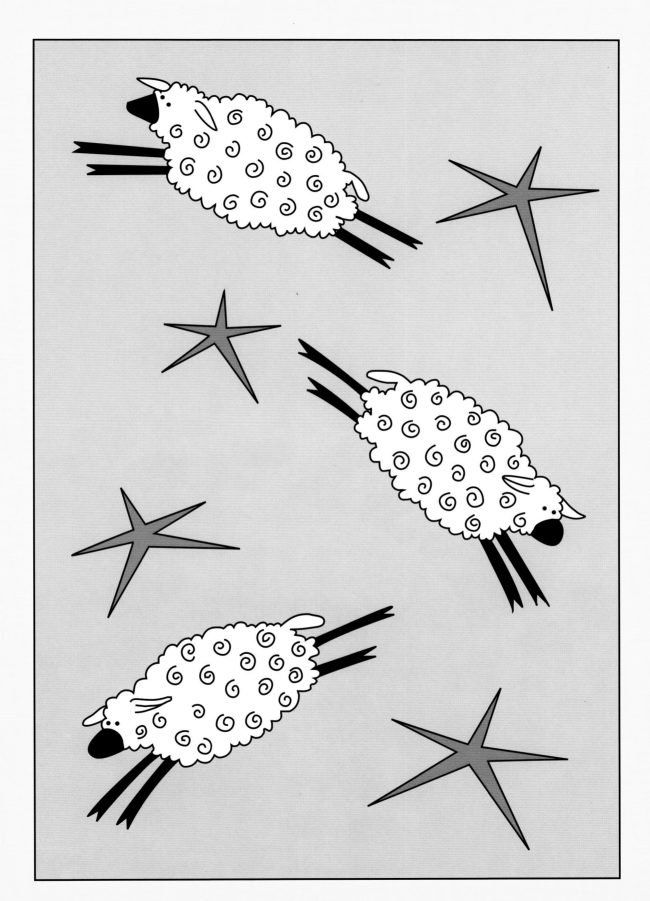

OUT TO LUNCH
PAINTING INSTRUCTIONS—

STUFF YOU GOTTA HAVE

Wooden plate, 14" diameter with
   2½" rim
Pure Pigment Paint Colors
   Burnt Sienna
   Ivory Black
   Titanium White
Acrylic Paint Colors
   Coastal Blue (sky blue)
   Cotton Candy (light pink)
   Clover (deep yellow green)
   Evergreen (medium green)
   School Bus Yellow (deep yellow)
   Tapioca (off white)
Clear acrylic spray
Brown paper bag or old cotton rag
Tracing paper
#2 lead pencil
Graphite paper
White graphite paper
Paper towels
Round brush, #4 or #5
Flat brush
Liner brush
Stylus
Polyurethane finish

DO IT LIKE THIS

1 Base-coat the plate front Tapioca and the entire back Ivory Black. Let the paint dry. Use a piece of brown paper bag or an old cotton rag to smooth the painted surfaces. Wipe off the sanding dust. (Acrylic paint often raises the grain of the wood.)

2 With tracing paper, duplicate the pattern. Turn the tracing over and rub over the pattern lines with a #2 lead pencil. You may transfer the design with a commercial graphite paper, but you'll want to eliminate messy excess graphite by wiping over the graphite with a paper towel.

3 Transfer the sky, ground, and cow outlines onto the plate. Mix Titanium White and Coastal Blue, 2:1, and fill in the sky. Paint the back hill Clover and the front hill with a 1:1 mixture of Evergreen and School Bus Yellow. Let the paint dry.

OUT TO LUNCH

PAINTING INSTRUCTIONS (CONTINUED)—

DO IT LIKE THIS (CONTINUED)

4 Paint the cow body, including the horns, Tapioca and the spots, hooves, and tail tip Ivory Black. Mix equal parts of Cotton Candy and Tapioca and fill in the udder and the cow's inner ear. Shade the edge of the udder with Cotton Candy and highlight the center area with Tapioca. Let the paint dry. Use a piece of brown paper bag or an old cotton rag to smooth the painted surfaces. Wipe off the sanding dust.

5 Transfer the pattern details with white graphite paper. Fill in the clouds with Titanium White. Mix equal parts of Evergreen, School Bus Yellow, and Tapioca. Use this mixture to add the "crop" lines to the back hill and the blades of grass to the front hill. Paint the grass in the cow's mouth with this same mixture. Add a few strokes of School Bus Yellow for highlights. Outline the blades of grass with Ivory Black.

6 For the fence, mix Titanium White and Burnt Sienna, 2:1, and fill in the posts. Shade the posts with Burnt Sienna. Outline each post with Ivory Black and add Ivory Black barbed wire.

7 Paint the eyes Titanium White. Dip the end of a stylus into Titanium White and dot the large pupil highlight. Without dipping the stylus back into the paint, dot the small iris highlight. Then, dip the stylus into the Titanium White and repeat the process for the opposite eye. Let the paint dry.

8 Paint the cow bell strap Burnt Sienna. Mix equal parts of Burnt Sienna and Titanium White and fill in the bell side, top, and ring. Add a bit more Titanium White to the mixture and paint the front of the bell. Shade the back edge of the bell with Burnt Sienna and highlight the top and right edge of the front with Titanium White. Add all remaining outlining and details with Ivory Black.

9 Apply clear acrylic spray to all wood surfaces. If you plan to use the plate for serving cookies, apply several coats of a good polyurethane finish. Once guests empty the plate, wipe off with a damp cloth. (Fruit and/or hot foods will damage the surface of the plate.)

OUT TO LUNCH
PATTERN—

Design:
Enlarge 120%

JOLLY JACK-O-LANTERNS
PAINTING INSTRUCTIONS—

STUFF YOU GOTTA HAVE

Wooden tray
Pure Pigment Paint Colors
   Dioxazine Purple
   Ivory Black
   Pure Orange
   Red Light
   Titanium White
   Yellow Ochre
Acrylic Paint Colors
   Evergreen (medium green)
Clear acrylic spray
Brown paper bag or old cotton rag
Tracing paper
#2 lead pencil
Graphite paper
White graphite paper
Paper towels
Round brush, #4 or #5
Flat brushes

DO IT LIKE THIS

1 Base-coat the entire tray, inside and out, Dioxazine Purple. Add a small amount of Titanium White to the brush to create a slightly marbled effect. Let the paint dry.

2 With tracing paper, duplicate the patterns. Turn the tracing over and rub over the pattern lines with a #2 lead pencil. You may transfer the design with a commercial graphite paper, but you'll want to eliminate messy excess graphite by wiping over the graphite with a paper towel.

3 Transfer the designs onto the bottom and the sides of the wooden tray with white graphite paper. Paint the lettering and the stars Yellow Ochre. Let the paint dry. Outline the stars with Ivory Black.

4 Base-coat the jack-o-lanterns Pure Orange. Let the paint dry. Paint the eyes, noses, and mouths Yellow Ochre. Highlight jack-o-lanterns with Red Light. Paint the stems Evergreen. Let the paint dry. Outline the jack-o-lanterns with Ivory Black and add details.

5 Base-coat the moons Titanium White. If necessary, apply a second coat. Let the paint dry. Outline the moons with Ivory Black. Apply clear acrylic spray to all wood surfaces.

JOLLY JACK-O-LANTERNS
PATTERNS—

Lettering & Stars:
Enlarge 125%

Design:
Enlarge 155%

STAR LITE,
STAR BRITE

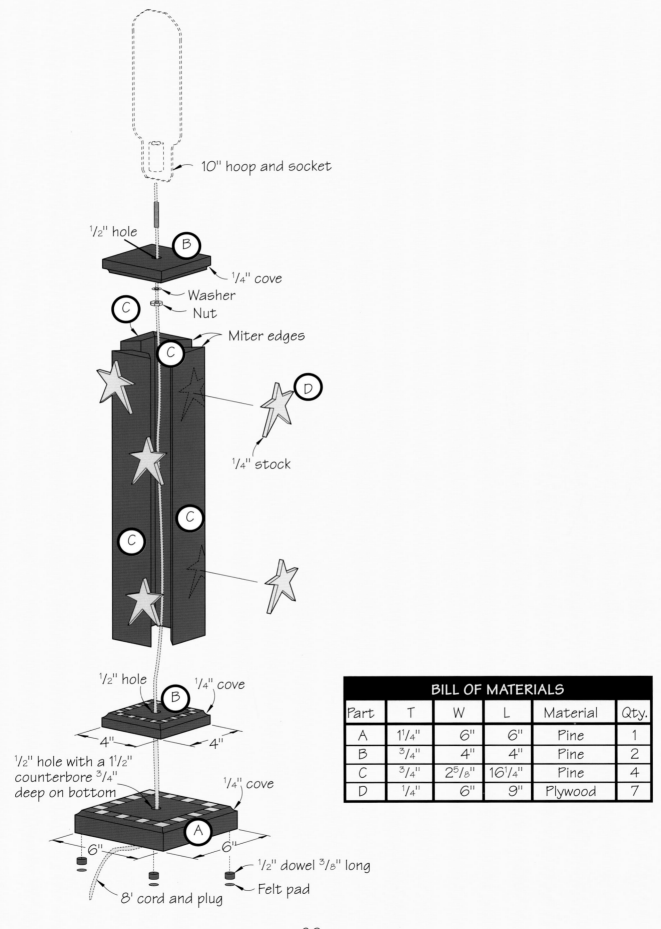

10" hoop and socket

¹/₂" hole

B

¹/₄" cove

Washer

Nut

C

C

Miter edges

D

¹/₄" stock

C

C

¹/₂" hole

¹/₄" cove

B

4"   4"

¹/₂" hole with a 1¹/₂"
counterbore ³/₄"
deep on bottom

¹/₄" cove

A

6"   6"

¹/₂" dowel ³/₈" long

Felt pad

8' cord and plug

BILL OF MATERIALS					
Part	T	W	L	Material	Qty.
A	1¹/₄"	6"	6"	Pine	1
B	³/₄"	4"	4"	Pine	2
C	³/₄"	2⁵/₈"	16¹/₄"	Pine	4
D	¹/₄"	6"	9"	Plywood	7

STAR LITE, STAR BRITE
WOODWORKING INSTRUCTIONS—

TOOLS & SUCH

Table saw
Router
Cove bit
Drill press
Band saw
Sandpaper, medium-grit and
    fine-grit
Tack cloth
Wood glue
10" hoop and socket
Washer and nut
8' electrical cord and plug
Cloth tape
Lamp shade

CUT IT OUT

1 Cut Parts A and B on the table saw; then add the cove detail with a router and the appropriate bit. Crosscut the four lamp sides (Part C) to length; then rip the miters on the table saw. Using the drill press, drill the 1½"-diameter counterbore on the underside of the base; then drill the ½"-diameter holes through the base and Part B.

2 For the stars, plane wood to ¼" thickness or use ¼" plywood. Draw an appropriate template, and cut the stars on the band saw,

preferably stacked and clamped so that you make all five at once, thereby ensuring they are identical in size and shape.

GET IT SANDED

1 Before assembly, make sure that all parts are finish sanded, with their sharp edges "killed" or slightly rounded, and that all tool marks are removed. Use a medium-grit sandpaper to sand the lamp and stars. Switch to a fine-grit sandpaper and sand again. Then lightly wipe over all surfaces with a tack cloth to pick up the dust created by sanding. (Don't firmly rub the tack cloth over the wood—the cloth will leave an unwanted tacky residue.)

PUT IT TOGETHER

1 Insert the lamp hoop and socket in the top (Part B), and fasten securely with the washer and nut. Thread the cord through the two base pieces (Parts A and B). Glue up the four mitered sides, using cloth tape to clamp them together. Make sure it is exactly square. Add the top and the two base parts. Once the glue has dried, use medium-grit and then fine-grit sandpaper to smooth the sharp vertical edges of the miters. You can now begin painting. When painting is finished, attach the stars. Finally, place the lamp shade on the lamp.

STAR LITE, STAR BRITE
PAINTING INSTRUCTIONS—

Acrylic Paint Colors
   Almond Parfait (gray skintone)
   Cherry Royale (cherry)
   Thunder Blue (navy)
Antiquing Medium
   Apple Butter Brown
Clear acrylic spray
Brown paper bag or old cotton rag
Ruler
#2 lead pencil
Round brush, #4 or #5
Flat brush
Woodburner, optional
Brass plumber's brush, optional
Tack cloth, optional
Wood glue
4 adhesive-backed felt pads

DO IT LIKE THIS

1 Measure in $5/8$" from the outer edges of the base board front and draw a pencil line. Use your pencil to draw the checks along the border. Make certain you have enough checks to alternate colors completely around the board. (Don't attempt to make the checks perfectly matched in width. Part of the charm of folk art is the lack of conformity in shapes and style.)

2 Use a woodburner to burn all penciled border lines. Continue the pattern on the sides of the board. If you've never used a woodburner, here are some important things to remember: Set the tip down and pull it toward you, following the pattern lines. For even lines, keep the tool moving at an even pace. To remove carbon buildup on the tip, use a brass plumber's brush. Use tack cloth to wipe away the woodburned particles.

If you prefer, paint the checks without burning the lines.

3 Paint all Cherry Royale checks and let the paint dry. Then paint the Almond Parfait checks. Next, paint the remaining lamp surfaces Thunder Blue, leaving a small spot unpainted where each star attaches. Paint the star fronts, edges, and all but the center of the backs Almond Parfait. Leave the center of the backs unpainted. (You'll get a much better bond with the glue if you glue raw wood to raw wood.) Let the paint dry. Use a piece of brown paper bag or an old cotton rag to smooth the painted surfaces. Wipe off the sanding dust. (Acrylic paint often raises the grain of the wood.)

4 With the tip of the woodburner, burn dots in each Cherry Royale check.

5 Sand the paint off the spots where the stars attach to the lamp. With wood glue, attach the stars to the lamp. Let the glue dry.

6 Antique all wood surfaces with Apple Butter Brown antiquing medium and let the antiquing dry.

7 Apply clear acrylic spray to all wood surfaces. Finally, place the lamp shade on the lamp. (To protect your furniture, we recommend using adhesive-backed felt pads on the bottom of the lamp feet.)

STAR LITE, STAR BRITE
PATTERN—

Star:
Reproduce 100%

SMILING
SUNFLOWERS

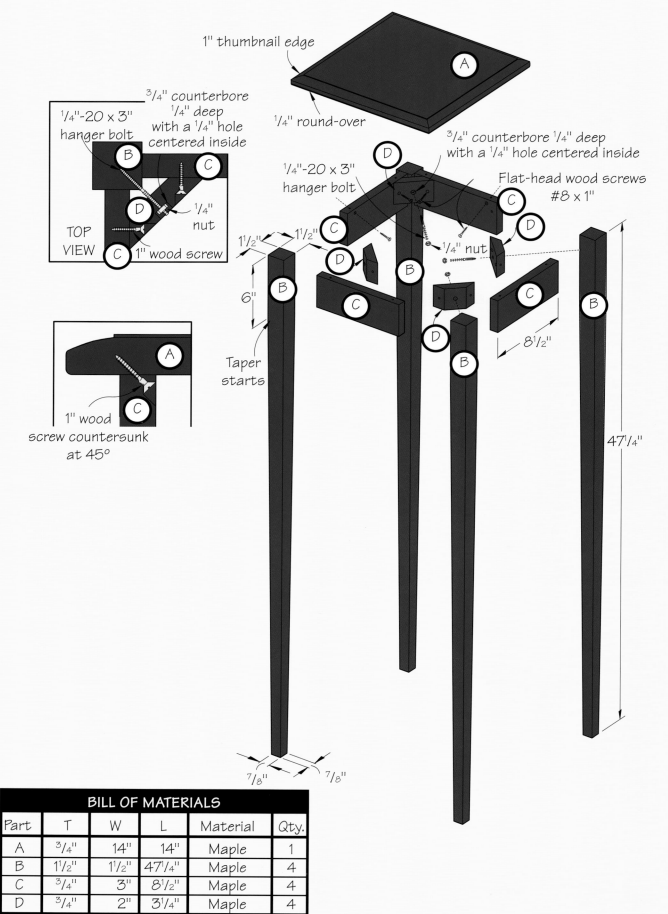

1" thumbnail edge

A

$^{1}/_{4}$" round-over

$^{3}/_{4}$" counterbore $^{1}/_{4}$" deep with a $^{1}/_{4}$" hole centered inside

$^{1}/_{4}$"-20 x 3" hanger bolt

B
C
D
$^{1}/_{4}$" nut
1" wood screw

TOP VIEW

$^{3}/_{4}$" counterbore $^{1}/_{4}$" deep with a $^{1}/_{4}$" hole centered inside

Flat-head wood screws #8 x 1"

$^{1}/_{4}$"-20 x 3" hanger bolt

$^{1}/_{4}$" nut

D
C
D
C
D
B
C
D
C
B

$1^{1}/_{2}$"
$1^{1}/_{2}$"
6"
B
Taper starts

8$^{1}/_{2}$"
B

47$^{1}/_{4}$"

A
1" wood screw countersunk at 45°
C

$^{7}/_{8}$"
$^{7}/_{8}$"

BILL OF MATERIALS					
Part	T	W	L	Material	Qty.
A	$^{3}/_{4}$"	14"	14"	Maple	1
B	$1^{1}/_{2}$"	$1^{1}/_{2}$"	47$^{1}/_{4}$"	Maple	4
C	$^{3}/_{4}$"	3"	8$^{1}/_{2}$"	Maple	4
D	$^{3}/_{4}$"	2"	3$^{1}/_{4}$"	Maple	4

SMILING SUNFLOWERS
WOODWORKING INSTRUCTIONS—

CUT IT OUT

1 Start by making the top (Part A), which is produced by edge gluing two or more boards to produce the desired 14" width. Depending on the stock available to you, you will edge-glue three 5"-wide boards, four 4" boards, or some other combination. Make sure the edges are as straight as your tools will permit, by joining them or ripping with great care on the table saw. Be careful that the clamping force is not so great that it causes the panel to curve or scoop across its width; a good way to prevent this is to "sandwich-clamp" either end of the panel between a pair of two-by-four blocks, each about as long as the panel is wide. Use a single thickness of newspaper to keep from gluing the two-by-fours to the panel (or the panel to your workbench!).

2 Once this top panel is complete, remove the excess glue with a scraper, and sand both faces flat using an abrasive planer, a 4" x 24" belt sander, or hand tools. Trim to dimension. The bevelled profile of the edge can be made in a single operation only by using a shaper with appropriate bit. If you do not have or have access to this tool, you can either modify the design to allow table saw milling, or hand-carve using a plane.

3 The legs in this project must taper from $1^{1}/_{2}$"-wide to $^{7}/_{8}$"-wide over a length of almost four feet. These are cut on the table saw using a tapering jig. After cutting, sand the legs smooth on the 6" x 48" belt sander, and hand-sand to finish, being careful to produce a slight round-over on each edge. Cut the apron pieces (Part C) and the corner blocks (Part D).

SMILING SUNFLOWERS
WOODWORKING INSTRUCTIONS (CONTINUED)—

CUT IT OUT (CONTINUED)

4 In the appropriate locations in each of the four corner blocks, drill shallow countersink holes. (These serve to hide the screw heads.) Because screws won't go into maple without pre-drilled holes, you must drill pilot holes completely through each block. These pilot holes start at the bottom of each countersink hole and their diameter is sized to allow the shank of the screw to pass through. Next, you must drill tapper holes into the apron pieces. To do this, align parts carefully and hold them in place with tape or clamps. Select a drill bit whose diameter is about half the diameter of the screw; then insert it through each corner block's countersink and pilot holes to drill a tapper hole into the apron.

GET IT SANDED

1 Before assembly, make sure that all parts are finish sanded, with their sharp edges "killed" or slightly rounded, and that all tool marks are removed. Use a medium-grit sandpaper to sand the table. Switch to a fine-grit sandpaper and sand again. Then lightly wipe over all surfaces with a tack cloth to pick up the dust created by sanding. (Don't firmly rub the tack cloth over the wood—the cloth will leave an unwanted tacky residue.)

PUT IT TOGETHER

1 Run through a dry assembly first, without glue, to be sure all parts fit. Glue up and assemble the base, making sure that when the screws are tightened, all parts are in proper alignment. Once the glue has dried, turn it upside down and drill the angled holes for the screws that will attach the top, then glue and screw it on. Once the glue has dried, you can begin painting.

SMILING SUNFLOWERS
PAINTING INSTRUCTIONS—

STUFF YOU GOTTA HAVE

Latex Acrylic Satin
  Hunter Green
Pure Pigment Paint Colors
  Ivory Black
  Pure Orange
Acrylic Paint Colors
  Clover (deep yellow green)
  Earthenware (rusty brown)
  Harvest Gold (deep gold)
  Molasses (medium brown)
  Old Ivy (deep green)
  Rusty Nail (rust)
  Tapioca (off white)
Clear acrylic spray
Brown paper bag or old cotton rag
Tracing paper
#2 lead pencil
Graphite paper
White graphite paper
Paper towels
Round brush, #4 or #5
Flat brush
Liner brush
Stylus

DO IT LIKE THIS

1 Mix equal parts of Rusty Nail and Pure Orange paint. Apply the mixture to the center square of the tabletop and to all four skirt (side) pieces. (Don't forget to paint the inside of the skirt and the underside of the center square on the stand top.)

2 Base-coat the legs and the beveled edge of the top with Hunter Green Latex Acrylic Satin paint. Continue painting the beveled area under the top edge up to the skirt piece. Use a piece of brown paper bag or an old cotton rag to smooth the painted surfaces. Wipe off the sanding dust. (Acrylic paint often raises the grain of the wood.)

3 With tracing paper, duplicate the sunflower pattern. Turn the tracing over and rub over the pattern lines with a #2 lead pencil. You may transfer the design with a commercial graphite paper, but you'll want to eliminate messy excess graphite by wiping over the graphite with a paper towel. Use white graphite paper to transfer the outlines to the sides of the table.

SMILING SUNFLOWERS
PAINTING INSTRUCTIONS (CONTINUED)—

DO IT LIKE THIS (CONTINUED)

4 Paint the stems Clover; then shade the upper part of the stem (the shadow from the flower) with Old Ivy. Paint the petals Harvest Gold. Base-coat the flower centers Earthenware; then blend in a bit of Molasses on the right side of each center oval. Let the paint dry. Now copy the facial features onto the base-coated flower centers with white graphite paper.

5 Paint the eyes Tapioca. Fill in the irises with Earthenware. Let the paint dry. Add Ivory Black pupils. Dip the end of a stylus into Tapioca and dot the large pupil highlight. Without dipping the stylus back into the paint, dot the small iris highlight. Then, dip the stylus into the Tapioca and repeat the process for the remaining eyes.

6 Thin Ivory Black with water until it's the consistency of ink and, using a small liner brush, paint the eyes, noses, mouths and petal veins, and outline all shapes. Let the paint dry.

7 Apply clear acrylic spray to all wood surfaces. Let the spray dry thoroughly and apply a second coat of clear acrylic spray. If you are painting the clay pot, repeat the painting instruction steps.

SMILING SUNFLOWERS
PATTERN—

Sunflowers:
Reproduce 100%

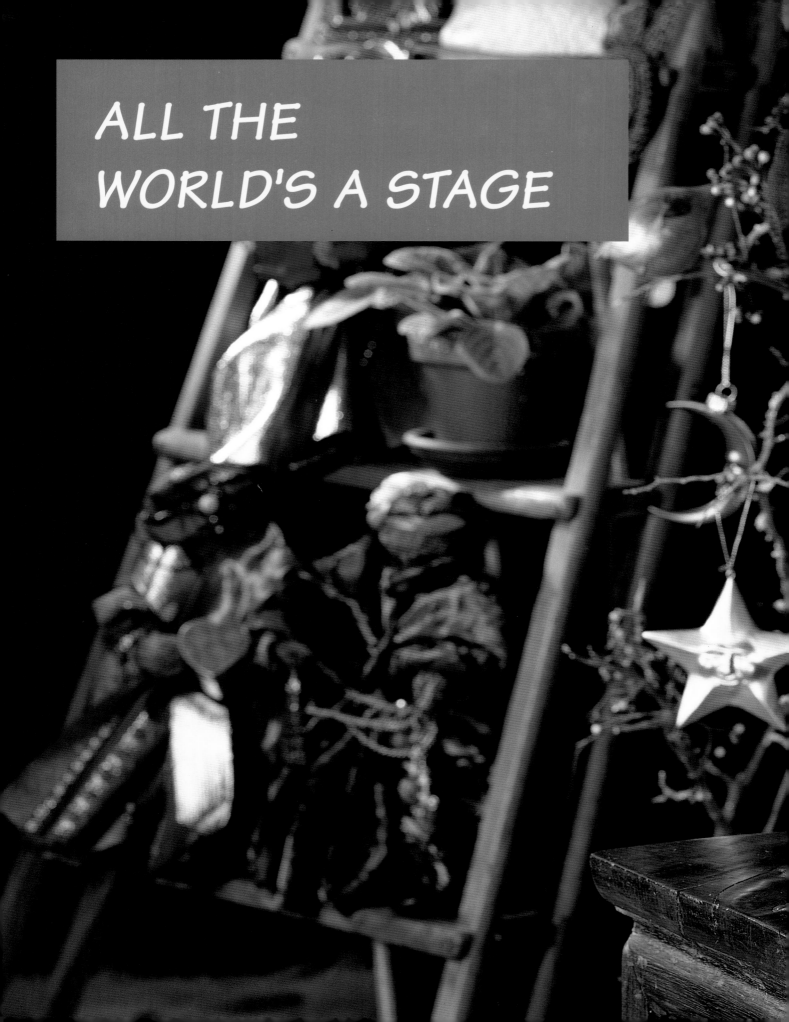

ALL THE
WORLD'S A STAGE

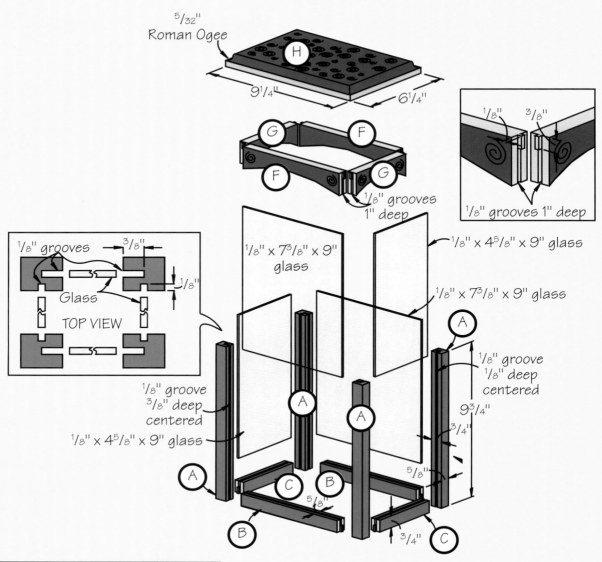

$^5/_{32}$" Roman Ogee

$9^1/_4$" $6^1/_4$"

H

G F

F G

$^1/_8$" grooves 1" deep

$^1/_8$" $^3/_8$"

$^1/_8$" grooves 1" deep

$^1/_8$" grooves $^3/_8$"

$^1/_8$"

Glass

TOP VIEW

$^1/_8$" x $7^3/_8$" x 9" glass

$^1/_8$" x 4$^5/_8$" x 9" glass

$^1/_8$" x 7$^3/_8$" x 9" glass

A

$^1/_8$" groove $^1/_8$" deep centered

A

9$^3/_4$"

$^3/_4$"

$^5/_8$"

$^1/_8$" groove $^3/_8$" deep centered

$^1/_8$" x 4$^5/_8$" x 9" glass

A

B

$^5/_8$"

C

$^3/_4$"

C

B

A

$^1/_8$" groove $^3/_8$" deep

A

$^3/_8$"

B

$^1/_8$"

$^1/_8$" x $^3/_8$" tenon

C

BILL OF MATERIALS					
Part	T	W	L	Material	Qty.
A	$^5/_8$"	$^3/_4$"	$9^3/_4$"	Pine	4
B	$^5/_8$"	$^3/_4$"	$7^3/_8$"	Pine	2
C	$^5/_8$"	$^3/_4$"	$4^5/_8$"	Pine	2
D	$^7/_8$"	$6^1/_2$"	$9^1/_2$"	Pine	1
E	$^1/_4$"	$4^3/_{16}$"	$7^3/_{16}$"	Pine	1
F	$^5/_8$"	$1^3/_8$"	$7^3/_8$"	Pine	2
G	$^5/_8$"	$1^3/_8$"	$4^5/_8$"	Pine	2
H	$^3/_4$"	$6^1/_4$"	$9^1/_4$"	Pine	1

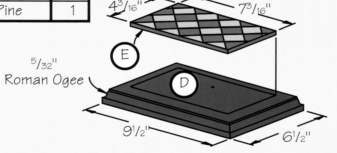

$4^3/_{16}$" $7^3/_{16}$"

E

$^5/_{32}$" Roman Ogee

D

$9^1/_2$" $6^1/_2$"

ALL THE WORLD'S A STAGE
WOODWORKING INSTRUCTIONS—

TOOLS & SUCH

Table saw
Shaper and Roman Ogee bit
Band saw
Files
Sandpaper, medium-grit and
    fine-grit
Tack cloth
Wood glue
Masking tape
Glass or acrylic sheets

CUT IT OUT

1 Start by making the sides (Part A) and the bottom (Parts B and C), all of which are identical in thickness and width. Cutting is simpler and quicker if the parts are made from two single pieces of stock, one about 40" long (to make the four sides) and one about 26" long (to make the four bottom pieces). Rip the appropriate grooves using the kerf of the table saw blade; then simply crosscut the longer pieces to length. Cut the four top rail pieces (Parts F and G) in a similar manner from stock $1\frac{1}{2}$"-wide; crosscut to length, then make the grooves.

2 The box is held together partly by small tenons that project from the ends of the bottom and top rail parts, and fit into grooves in the sides. These tenons are $\frac{1}{8}$"-thick, $\frac{3}{8}$"-wide, and long enough to fit comfortably in their grooves with $\frac{1}{8}$" of their length projecting. To cut these small parts, rip a piece of scrap to $\frac{1}{8}$" x $\frac{3}{8}$", then crosscut to length.

3 The top and bottom (Parts H and D) are slightly different in dimension, and are made by running the edges of the stock through a shaper with the appropriate "Roman Ogee" bit. The curved detailing on the underside of the top rails (Parts F and G) is cut using a band saw, and the saw cuts are then cleaned up with files and hand sanding.

GET IT SANDED

1 Before assembly, make sure that all parts are finish sanded, with their sharp edges "killed" or slightly rounded, and that all tool marks are removed. Use a medium-grit sandpaper to sand the saw-cut pieces. Switch to a fine-grit sandpaper and sand again. Then lightly wipe over all surfaces with a tack cloth to pick up the dust created by sanding. (Don't firmly rub the tack cloth over the wood—the cloth will leave an unwanted tacky residue.)

ALL THE WORLD'S A STAGE
WOODWORKING INSTRUCTIONS (CONTINUED)—

PUT IT TOGETHER

1 Run through a dry assembly first, without glue, to be sure all parts fit. Glue up the tenons in place on parts B, C, F, and G, making sure that they do not project so far that they won't fit snugly into their respective grooves. Now you are ready to size the glass. Make a dry assembly, without glue, of the sides and the bottom, and hold it together with tape. The width of your glass panels should be the same as the length of the bottom, Parts B and C, plus their two projecting tenons. Since glass is both impossible to trim and somewhat costly, it is wise to have the glass cut about

$\frac{1}{16}$" less than your measurements. As an alternative, consider using acrylic sheets, available in most plastic or hobby shops, which you can both cut on your table saw and sand to fit as needed.

2 Using the glass or acrylic sheets, run through the assembly process again, without glue, until you are confident that all parts fit and align properly. Then make the final assembly, but do not install the glass or acrylic sheets, the side arches, or the top. Once the glue has dried, you can begin painting. When painting is finished, install the glass or acrylic sheets, the side arches, and the top.

Top

Base

102

ALL THE WORLD'S A STAGE
PAINTING INSTRUCTIONS—

STUFF YOU GOTTA HAVE

Pure Pigment Paint Colors
   Napthol Crimson
   Ultramarine Blue
Acrylic Paint Colors
   School Bus Yellow (deep yellow)
Antiquing Medium
   Apple Butter Brown
Clear acrylic spray
Gold marker
   with extra-fine point
Brown paper bag or old cotton rag
Tracing paper
#2 lead pencil
Graphite paper
Paper towels
Round brush, #4 or #5
Flat brush
Stylus

DO IT LIKE THIS

1 Paint the routered base, the edges of the raised base panel, the side arches, and the top Ultramarine Blue. Let the paint dry. Use a piece of brown paper bag or an old cotton rag to smooth the painted surfaces. Wipe off the sanding dust. (Acrylic paint often raises the grain of the wood.)

2 On tracing paper, draw a grid of 1" squares. Turn the tracing over and rub over the pattern lines with a #2 lead pencil. You may transfer the design with a commercial graphite paper, but you'll want to eliminate messy excess graphite by wiping over the graphite with a paper towel.

3 Paint the raised panel on the base School Bus Yellow. Let the paint dry. Transfer the pattern onto the raised panel on the base turning the grid to form an "argyle" pattern. Paint alternating squares Napthol Crimson to create a checkerboard effect. Let the paint dry. Paint the sides of the raised panel on the base School Bus Yellow. Paint the pieces that will frame the glass panels Napthol Crimson. Let the paint dry. Antique the painted surfaces with Apple Butter Brown antiquing medium and let the antiquing dry.

4 Apply clear acrylic spray to all wood surfaces. Using the gold marker, draw the spirals on the top and on the side arches, and outline the diamonds on the base. Do not apply any finish once you've added the gold details. Finally, install the glass or acrylic sheets, the side arches, and the top.

NEVER
ENOUGH THYME

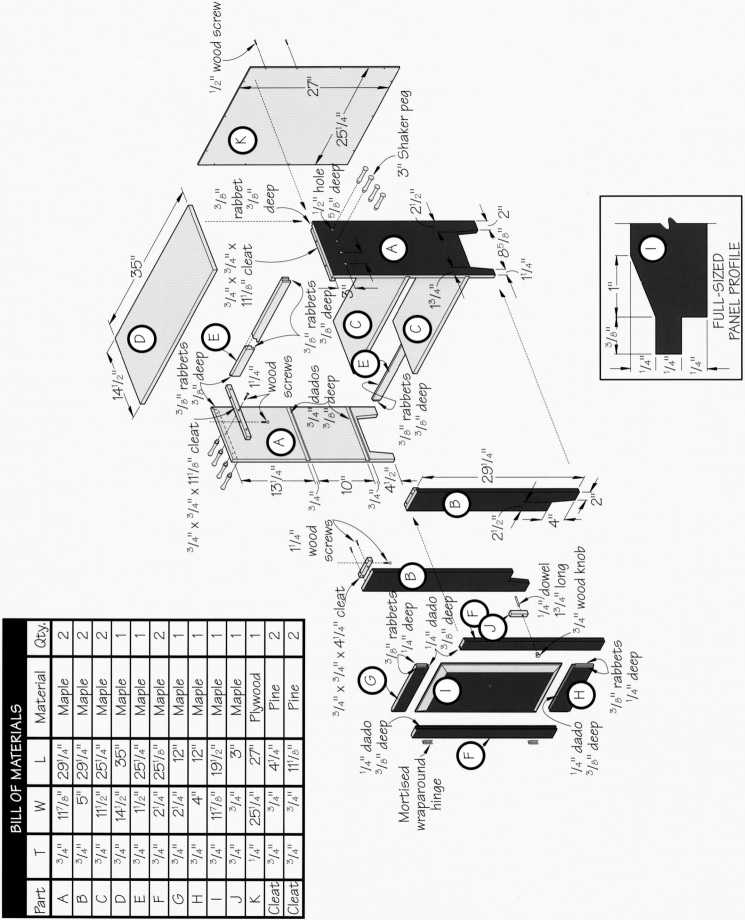

½" wood screw

27"

25¼"

K

3/8" rabbet
3/8" deep

35"

½" hole
5/8" deep

3" Shaker peg

2½"

2"

8⁵/₈"

1¼"

A

3/4" x 3/4" x 11⅛" cleat

D

14½"

E

3/8" rabbets
3/8" deep

5"

3"

13¾"

C

C

E

3/8" rabbets
3/8" deep

FULL-SIZED
PANEL PROFILE

I

3/8"

1"

1/4"

1/4"

1/4"

1¼" wood
screws

A

3/4" dados
3/8" deep

13¼"

3/4"

10"

3/4"

4½"

3/4" x 3/4" x 11⅛" cleat

29¼"

B

2½"

4"

2"

1¼" wood
screws

B

3/4" x 3/4" x 4¼" cleat

3/8" rabbets
1/4" deep

1/4" dado
3/8" deep

F

J

1/4" dowel
13/4" long

3/4" wood knob

G

1/4" dado
3/8" deep

I

H

3/8" rabbets
1/4" deep

Mortised
wraparound
hinge

F

1/4" dado
3/8" deep

BILL OF MATERIALS

NEVER ENOUGH THYME

WOODWORKING INSTRUCTIONS—

TOOLS & SUCH

Table saw
4 two-by-four blocks
Newspaper
Scraper
Abrasive planer or
    4" x 24" belt sander
Band saw
Files
Shaper or plane
Drill
Drill bits
Sandpaper, medium-grit and
    fine-grit
Tack cloth
Wood glue
2 wraparound hinges
14 flat-head wood screws,
    #6 x $^1/_2$" long
10 flat-head wood screws,
    #8 x $1^1/_4$" long
Screwdriver
Dowel, $^1/_4$" diameter, $1^3/_4$" long
Wooden knob, $^3/_4$"
8 Shaker pegs, 3"

CUT IT OUT

1 Start by making the sides (Part A), the door panel (Part I), the shelves (Part C) and the top (Part D). Each of these parts will be made by edge gluing two or more boards to produce the desired width. Since the sides are to

be painted, they can be made from $^3/_4$" paint-grade hardwood veneer plywood instead of solid maple. The shelves (Part C) can also be plywood; simply apply iron-on maple wood tape to the front edge.

2 Part D, the top, for example, needs a finished width of $14^1/_2$". Depending on the stock available to you, you will edge-glue three 5"-wide boards, four 4" boards, or some other combination. Make sure the edges are as straight as your tools will permit, by joining them or ripping with great care on the table saw. Be careful that the clamping force is not so great that it causes the panel to curve or scoop across its width; a good way to prevent this is to "sandwich-clamp" either end of the panel between a pair of two-by-four blocks, each about as long as the panel is wide. Use a single thickness of newspaper to keep from gluing the two-by-fours to the panel (or the panel to your workbench!).

3 Once these panels are complete, remove the excess glue with a scraper, and sand both faces flat using an abrasive planer, a 4" x 24" belt sander, or hand tools. Trim to dimension. On each of the two sides (Part A), cut out the space between the feet using a band saw. The saw cuts are then cleaned up with files and hand sanding. Do likewise for the front legs (Part B).

NEVER ENOUGH THYME
WOODWORKING INSTRUCTIONS (CONTINUED)—

CUT IT OUT (CONTINUED)

4 The rabbets and dados are cut using a dado blade on the table saw. (Maple is a hardwood, so best results will be achieved by using carbide-tipped blades throughout.) Because of the shape of the door panel, its bevel can be made in a single operation only by using a shaper with appropriate bit. If you do not have or have access to this tool, you can either modify the design to allow table saw cutting, or hand-carve using a plane.

5 Attach the cleats to the tops of the sides (Part A) and the front legs (Part B). Make sure the holes going through these cleats, which will eventually hold the screws fastening the top, are properly sized to allow the screws to pass through, and set far enough out (or slightly angled) so that you can get your hand and a screwdriver in to attach them.

GET IT SANDED

1 Before assembly, make sure that all parts are finish sanded, with their sharp edges "killed" or slightly rounded, and that all tool marks are removed. Use a medium-grit sandpaper to sand the cabinet. Switch to a fine-grit sandpaper and sand again. Then lightly wipe over all surfaces with a tack cloth to pick up the dust created by sanding. (Don't firmly rub the tack cloth over the wood—the cloth will leave an unwanted tacky residue.)

PUT IT TOGETHER

1 Run through a dry assembly first, without glue, to be sure all parts fit. Glue up the door, then glue up the carcase with back. Once the glue has dried, you can begin painting. When painting is finished, add the Shaker pegs. Install the wooden knob and add the hinges. Attach the door, the latch, and the top.

NEVER ENOUGH THYME

PAINTING INSTRUCTIONS—

STUFF YOU GOTTA HAVE

Latex Acrylic Satin
  Hunter Green
Acrylic Paint Colors
  Buttercrunch (light beige)
  Sunset Orange (burnt orange)
Clear acrylic spray
Wood sealer
Masking tape
Brown paper bag or old cotton rag
Tracing paper
#2 lead pencil
Graphite paper
White graphite paper
Paper towels
Round brush, #4 or #5
Flat brush

DO IT LIKE THIS

1 Mask off the edge of the cabinet interior with masking tape. Seal the inside of the cabinet, the Shaker pegs, the wooden knob, and the top with wood sealer according to manufacturer's instructions. Let the sealer dry. Use a piece of brown paper bag or an old cotton rag to smooth the sealed surfaces. Wipe off the sanding dust. (Sealer often raises the grain of the wood.) Remove the masking tape.

2 Mask off the bevel in the door. Base-coat the sides and front of the cabinet with Hunter Green.

Paint the frame of the door and the door insert panel with Hunter Green Latex Acrylic Satin paint. Repeat on the inside of the door and panel. Leave the door hardware unpainted. Let the paint dry. Use a piece of brown paper bag or an old cotton rag to smooth the painted surfaces. Wipe off the sanding dust. (Acrylic paint often raises the grain of the wood.)

3 With tracing paper, duplicate the patterns. Turn the tracing over and rub over the pattern lines with a #2 lead pencil. You may transfer the design with a commercial graphite paper, but you'll want to eliminate messy excess graphite by wiping over the graphite with a paper towel.

4 Transfer the design onto the door insert panel and the corner motifs with white graphite paper. Paint the lettering and the corner motifs Buttercrunch. Paint the "box" around the letter "N" and the dots Sunset Orange. Let the paint dry.

5 Apply clear acrylic spray to the interior and the exterior of the cabinet. Finally, add the Shaker pegs, install the wooden knob, and add the hinges. Attach the door, the latch, and the top.

NEVER ENOUGH THYME

PATTERNS—

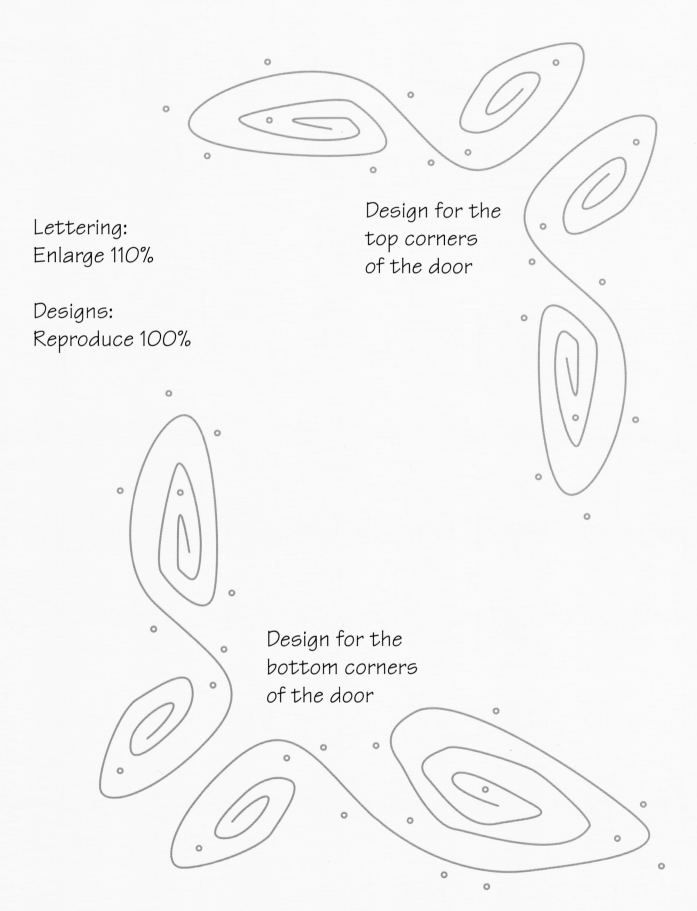

Lettering:
Enlarge 110%

Designs:
Reproduce 100%

Design for the
top corners
of the door

Design for the
bottom corners
of the door

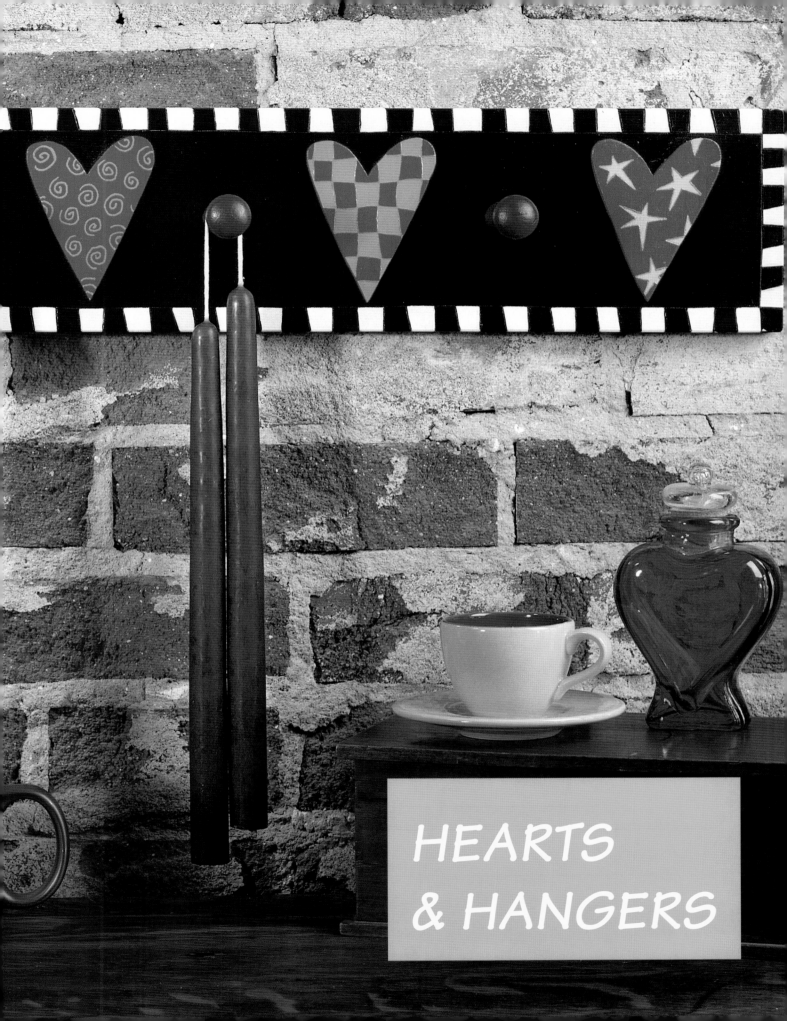

HEARTS
& HANGERS

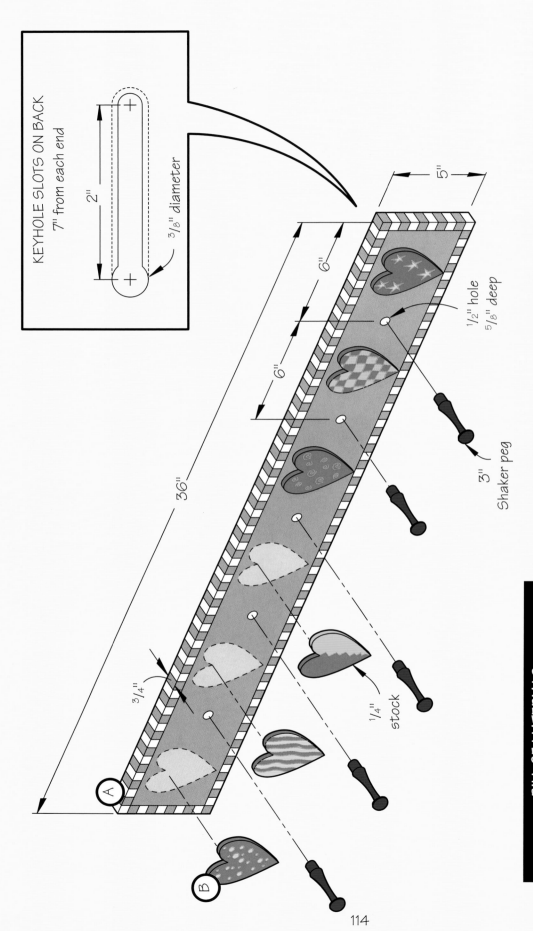

KEYHOLE SLOTS ON BACK
7" from each end

2"

³/₈" diameter

5"

6"

6"

½" hole
⁵/₈" deep

3"
Shaker peg

36"

³/₄"

¼"
stock

A

B

BILL OF MATERIALS

Part	T	W	L	Material	Qty.
A	³/₄"	5"	36"	Pine	1
B	¼"	6"	9"	Pine	6

HEARTS & HANGERS
WOODWORKING INSTRUCTIONS—

TOOLS & SUCH

Band saw
Plane
Router and keyhole bit or
   chisel
Drill or drill press
Drill bits
Sandpaper, medium-grit and
   fine-grit
Tack cloth
Wood glue
5 Shaker pegs, 3"

CUT IT OUT

1 The mounting board is made of any available 3/4"-thick stock, such as pine. For the hearts, plane pine to 1/4" thickness or use 1/4" plywood. Draw an appropriate template, and cut the hearts on the band saw, preferably stacked and clamped so that you make all six at once, thereby ensuring they are identical in size and shape.

2 The purpose of the keyhole slots on the back of the mounting board is to permit easy installation on a wall. The simplest way to mill this slot is with a router and a keyhole bit. However, a fair amount of time and skill is needed to create the appropriate router jig and setup to make this cut.

Therefore, a router is only worth using if you have a lot of time, or if you plan to make more than one coatrack. One alternative is to find and attach an appropriate piece of hanger hardware. Another is to use a chisel to cut two larger mortises, about 1"-wide, 1/2" deep, and 2" long. Then cut two rabbeted rails about 1 3/4" long and glue them securely in the larger mortises to achieve the same keyhole profile. The holes for the Shaker pegs are drilled with a hand drill or drill press.

GET IT SANDED

1 Before assembly, make sure that all parts are finish sanded, with their sharp edges "killed" or slightly rounded, and that all tool marks are removed. Use a medium-grit sandpaper to sand the mounting board and hearts. Switch to a fine-grit sandpaper and sand again. Then lightly wipe over all surfaces with a tack cloth to pick up the dust created by sanding. (Don't firmly rub the tack cloth over the wood—the cloth will leave an unwanted tacky residue.)

PUT IT TOGETHER

1 You can now begin painting. When painting is finished, glue the hearts in place, being careful to make sure they are evenly spaced and aligned; then install the Shaker pegs.

HEARTS & HANGERS
PAINTING INSTRUCTIONS—

STUFF YOU GOTTA HAVE

Pure Pigment Paint Colors
   Cerulean Blue Hue
   Ivory Black
   Napthol Crimson
   Pure Orange
   Titanium White
Acrylic Paint Colors
   School Bus Yellow (deep yellow)
Clear acrylic spray
Gold marker
   with extra-fine point
Brown paper bag or old cotton rag
Ruler
#2 lead pencil
Paper towels
Round brush, #4 or #5
Flat brush
Woodburner, optional
Brass plumber's brush, optional
Tack cloth, optional
Wood glue
Clamps

DO IT LIKE THIS

1 Measure in ³/₄" from the outer edges of the board front and draw a pencil line. Use your pencil to draw the checks along the border. Make certain you have enough checks to alternate colors completely around the board.

(Don't attempt to make the checks perfectly matched in width. Part of the charm of folk art is the lack of conformity in shapes and style.)

2 Use a woodburner to burn all penciled border lines. Continue the pattern on the sides of the board. If you've never used a woodburner, here are some important things to remember: Set the tip down and pull it toward you, following the pattern lines. For even lines, keep the tool moving at an even pace. To remove carbon buildup on the tip, use a brass plumber's brush. Use tack cloth to wipe away the woodburned particles.

   If you prefer, paint the checks without burning the lines.

3 Paint all Titanium White checks and let the paint dry. Then paint the Ivory Black checks. Next, paint the board center Ivory Black, leaving a small spot unpainted where each heart attaches. (You'll get a much better bond with the glue if you glue raw wood to raw wood.) Let the front dry thoroughly; then immediately turn the board over and paint the board back Ivory Black. With a narrow board of this length, if you leave the back unpainted, you invite board warpage. The moisture content in the piece of wood you purchase may vary greatly from one lumber company to the next. Sealing only one surface with paint means that the untreated side continues to dry out and shrink, thus causing the board to bend in shape. Let the back dry thoroughly. Use a piece of brown paper bag or an old cotton rag to smooth the painted surfaces. Wipe off the sanding dust. (Acrylic paint often raises the grain of the wood.)

4 Paint only the edges and fronts of the hearts. Do not add the gold marker details until instructed. Begin with the left heart. Heart 1: Base-coat with Napthol Crimson, and then add Pure Orange spots. Heart 2: Paint the edges Napthol Crimson and the alternating stripes Napthol Crimson and School Bus Yellow. Heart 3: Paint the left half and the left edges Napthol Crimson. Paint the right half and the right edges Pure Orange. Heart 4: Base-coat with Napthol Crimson. Heart 5: Paint the edges Napthol Crimson and the front with alternating checks of Napthol Crimson and Pure Orange. Heart 6: Base-coat with Napthol Crimson, and then paint School Bus Yellow stars. (You may need two coats of yellow for good coverage.) Let the painted hearts dry thoroughly. Use a piece of brown paper bag or an old cotton rag to smooth the painted surfaces. Wipe off the sanding dust.

5 Paint all Shaker pegs Cerulean Blue Hue. Do not paint the end of the pegs that glue into the board. With wood glue and clamps (be careful not to scratch the paint), attach the hearts to the board. Install the Shaker pegs in the board. Let the glue dry and remove the clamps.

6 Apply clear acrylic spray to all wood surfaces. Using the gold marker, add the remaining details to each heart. Do not apply any finish once you've added the gold details.

HEARTS & HANGERS

PATTERNS—

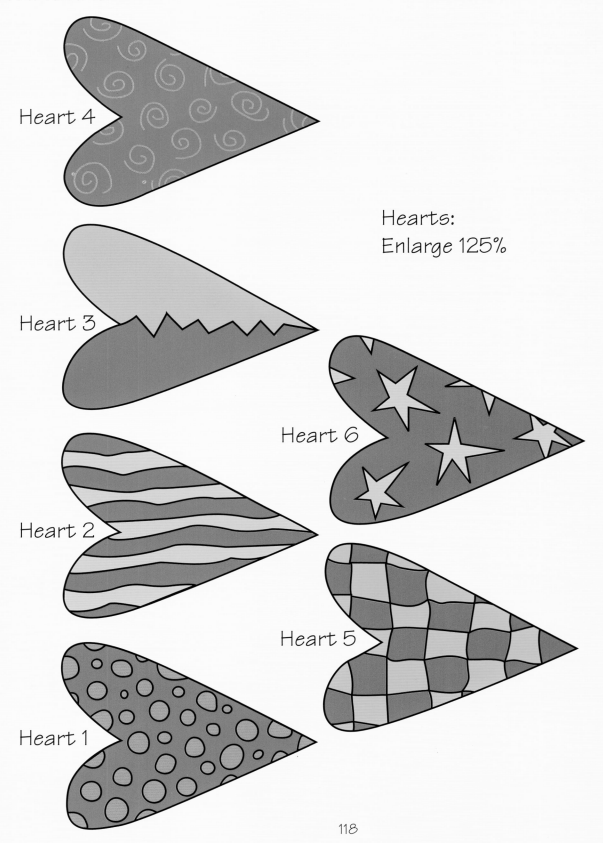

Heart 4

Hearts:
Enlarge 125%

Heart 3

Heart 6

Heart 2

Heart 5

Heart 1

TREASURE OF A CHEST

PATTERNS—

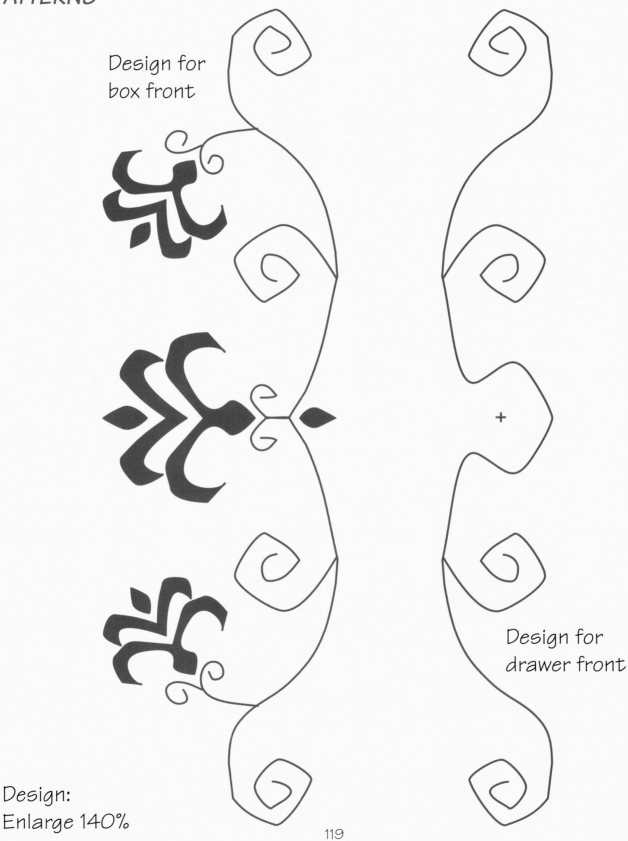

Design for
box front

Design for
drawer front

Design:
Enlarge 140%

TREASURE OF A CHEST

BILL OF MATERIALS

Part	T	W	L	Material	Qty.
A	1/2"	6 1/8"	7"	Pine	2
B	1/2"	7"	13"	Pine	1
C	1/2"	5 1/8"	13"	Pine	1
D	1/2"	5 5/8"	13"	Pine	1
E	1/2"	4 1/2"	13"	Pine	1
F	1/2"	6 1/8"	14"	Pine	1
G	1/4"	5 1/8"	13"	Pine	1
H	1/2"	2"	15"	Pine	2
I	1/2"	2"	7 1/8"	Pine	2
J	1/2"	1 5/8"	5 1/4"	Pine	2
K	1/2"	1 5/8"	11 13/16"	Pine	1
L	1/2"	1 15/16"	13"	Pine	1
M	1/8"	5 1/4"	12 7/8"	Hardboard	1
N	1/2"	1/2"	15"	Pine	2
O	1/2"	1/2"	7 1/8"	Pine	1

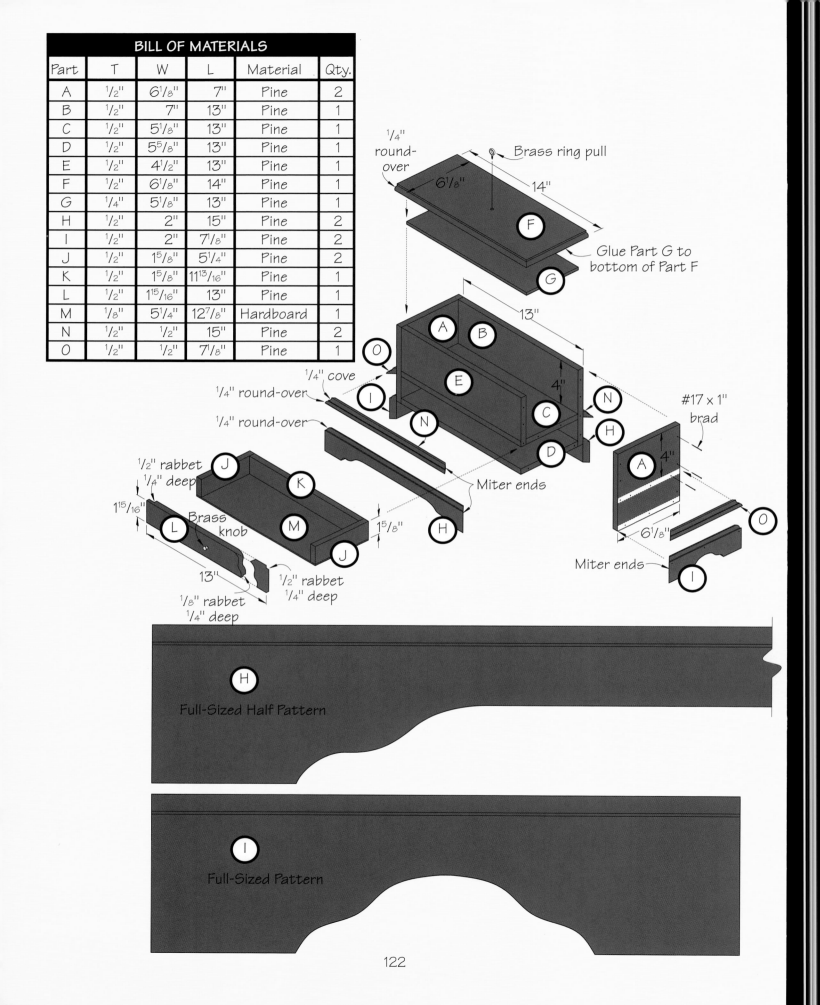

1/4" round-over

Brass ring pull

6 1/8"

14"

F

Glue Part G to bottom of Part F

G

13"

A B

E

4"

O

1/4" cove

1/4" round-over

I

1/4" round-over

N

C

N

H

D

Miter ends

N

#17 x 1" brad

A 4"

6 1/8"

O

Miter ends

I

1/2" rabbet
1/4" deep

J

K

1 15/16"

L Brass knob

M

J

1 5/8"

H

1/2" rabbet
1/4" deep

13"

1/8" rabbet
1/4" deep

H

Full-Sized Half Pattern

I

Full-Sized Pattern

122

TREASURE OF A CHEST
WOODWORKING INSTRUCTIONS—

TOOLS & SUCH

Table saw
Router
Cove bit
Band saw
Files
Sandpaper, medium-grit and
   fine-grit
Tack cloth
Wood glue
26 brads, #17 x 1"
Brass ring pull
Brass knob

CUT IT OUT

1 Except for Part G, the lid liner, and Part M, the drawer bottom, all the parts for this project are made from 1/2"-thick pine. The drawer front, Part L, is rabbeted to fit on the drawer body, and the four skirt pieces, Parts H and I, and the moulding trim, Parts N and O, are mitered; the remaining parts are as-sembled using simple butt joints.

2 Cut and dimension all parts on the table saw. The moulding trim, Parts N and O, may be milled using a router with a cove bit, or you can purchase an appropriate pre-milled moulding at any good millwork supply store. The curved pattern on the under-

side of the skirt (Parts H and I) is cut using a band saw, and the saw cuts are then cleaned up with files and hand sanding. The miters on the skirt and moulding are cut on the table saw using the miter fence set at 45 degrees.

GET IT SANDED

1 Before assembly, make sure that all parts are finish sanded, with their sharp edges "killed" or slightly rounded, and that all tool marks are removed. Use a medium-grit sandpaper to sand the saw-cut pieces. Switch to a fine-grit sandpaper and sand again. Then lightly wipe over all surfaces with a tack cloth to pick up the dust created by sanding. (Don't firmly rub the tack cloth over the wood—the cloth will leave an unwanted tacky residue.)

PUT IT TOGETHER

1 Run through a dry assembly first, without glue, to be sure all parts fit. Glue up the drawer; then glue the lid liner to the underside of the lid. Glue up the carcase without the mitered skirt. The brads act as clamps. Once the glue has dried, add the moulding trim and the skirt. You can now begin painting. When painting is finished, insert the drawer and sand as needed to make sure it fits well. Attach the brass ring pull and knob.

TREASURE OF A CHEST

PAINTING INSTRUCTIONS—

STUFF YOU GOTTA HAVE

Pure Pigment Paint Colors
  Titanium White
Acrylic Paint Colors
  Cherry Royale (cherry)
  Maple Syrup (deep brown)
  Rusty Nail (rust)
  Plantation Green
    (medium blue green)
Rosewood wood stain
Clear acrylic spray
Wood sealer
Brown paper bag or old cotton rag
Tracing paper
#2 lead pencil
Graphite paper
Paper towels
Round brush, #3, #4, or #5
Flat brush
Stylus

DO IT LIKE THIS

1 Stain the entire lid with Rosewood wood stain. Let the stain dry thoroughly while you paint the chest.

2 Base-coat all parts of the drawer and the chest Plantation Green. Let the paint dry. Use a piece of brown paper bag or an old cotton rag to smooth the painted surfaces. Wipe off the sanding dust. (Acrylic paint often raises the grain of the wood.) If necessary, apply another coat of Plantation Green. Let the second coat dry.

3 With tracing paper, duplicate the patterns. Turn the tracing over and rub over the pattern lines with a #2 lead pencil. You may transfer the design with a commercial graphite paper, but you'll want to eliminate messy excess graphite by wiping over the graphite with a paper towel.

4 Transfer the designs onto the chest and drawer fronts. Mix equal parts of Maple Syrup, Rusty Nail, and Cherry Royale. With a round brush (a #3, #4, or #5 works great), fill in the design lines. Let the paint dry. Lighten the mixture by adding a small amount of Titanium White.

5 Dip the small end of a stylus into the lighter mixture and apply small dots evenly along the design lines. For the larger areas of the design—the diamonds—outline the shapes with dots, then add a dot to the center. Let the paint dry.

6 Use a piece of brown paper bag or an old cotton rag to smooth the stained surfaces of the lid. Wipe off the sanding dust. Seal the lid with wood sealer according to manufacturer's instructions, allowing the lid top to dry before sealing the lid underside. Lightly sand with a piece of brown paper bag or an old cotton rag and wipe off the sanding dust. Add three or four more coats of wood sealer to both sides of the lid.

7 Apply clear acrylic spray. Finally, insert the drawer and sand as needed to make sure it fits well. Attach the brass ring pull and knob.

HOLIDAY SPIRITS

HOLIDAY SPIRITS
PAINTING INSTRUCTIONS—

Christmas Cheer Box:
Wine box
Pure Pigment Paint Colors
   Ivory Black
   Napthol Crimson
   Titanium White
Acrylic Paint Colors
   Harvest Gold (deep gold)
   Promenade (coral pink)
   School Bus Yellow (deep yellow)
   Sunset Orange (burnt orange)
   Victorian Rose (light skintone)
Clear acrylic spray
Sandpaper, fine-grit
Tack cloth
Tracing paper
White graphite paper
#2 lead pencil
Round brush, #4 or #5
Flat brush
Liner brush
Stylus

Happy New Year Box:
Wine box
Pure Pigment Paint Colors
   Ultramarine Blue
Acrylic Paint Colors
   Buttercrunch (light beige)
Metallic Colors
   Amethyst
   Inca Gold
   Rose Shimmer
Clear acrylic spray
Gold marker
   with extra-fine point
Sandpaper, fine-grit
Tack cloth
Tracing paper
White graphite paper
#2 lead pencil
Round brush, #4 or #5
Flat brush, #2
Liner brush
Stylus

DO IT LIKE THIS

1 Sand the entire box with fine-grit sandpaper. Then lightly wipe over all surfaces with a tack cloth to pick up the dust created by sanding. (Don't firmly rub the tack cloth over the wood—the cloth will leave an unwanted tacky residue.)

Christmas Cheer Box:

2 With tracing paper, duplicate the patterns. Base-coat the entire box, inside and out, with Napthol Crimson. Let the paint dry. Sand with fine-grit sandpaper and wipe off the sanding dust. Apply another coat of Napthol Crimson.

3 Transfer the lettering and the ribbon and bell designs onto the box with white graphite paper. Paint the lettering Victorian Rose. For the ribbon and bell motif on the box front, begin by filling in all of the shapes with Victorian Rose. Transfer the details for the bells and for the bends in the ribbon. Mix equal parts of Victorian Rose and Promenade. Working one loop of the bow at a time, paint the area with the mixture. Before the color dries, blend in Promenade in the shadow areas (behind the bells and on the back side of a twist or loop). Shade the darkest ribbon areas with a 2:1 mixture of Victorian Rose and Sunset Orange. Next, fill in the bells with a 2:1 mixture of Harvest Gold and School Bus Yellow. Let the paint dry. Mix equal parts of Harvest Gold, School Bus Yellow, and Sunset Orange and re-coat the two left bells. Before the paint dries, dab a bit of Sunset Orange on the darkest area of each bell and a touch of Titanium White on the lower right edge. Pat blend slightly. Shade the upper right bell in the same manner, except add a bit more Titanium White to the right side of the bell so that this bell has an overall lighter color than the other bells. Slightly thin Sunset Orange with water and paint the bell openings. Mix equal parts of Ivory Black and Sunset Orange and shade around the openings. Thin the mixture with water to make a transparent wash and apply the wash over the shaded areas of each bell. Dab off the excess paint with a cloth. (This works like an antiquing medium on the bells.) With the same thinned mixture, outline the darkest edges of the bells. Thin Titanium White with water until it's the consistency of ink. Dab a highlight on and outline the upper right edges of the upper bells and the lower right edge of the lower bell. Let the paint dry.

4 Apply clear acrylic spray to all wood surfaces. To prevent the lid from sticking to the box, let the paint and the acrylic spray dry for several days before inserting it into the box.

Happy New Year Box:

2 With tracing paper, duplicate the patterns. Base-coat the entire box, inside and out, with Ultramarine Blue. Let the paint dry. Sand with fine-grit sandpaper and wipe off the sanding dust. Apply another coat of Ultramarine Blue.

3 Transfer the lettering and stars onto the box with white graphite paper. Paint the lettering and stars Buttercrunch. With a #2 flat brush, make 3/8"-long random confetti strokes with the metallic colors: Amethyst, Inca Gold, and Rose Shimmer.

4 Apply clear acrylic spray to all wood surfaces. To prevent the lid from sticking to the box, let the paint and the acrylic spray dry for several days before inserting it into the box. Finally, using the gold marker, dot the lettering and outline the stars. Do not apply any finish once you've added the gold details.

HOLIDAY SPIRITS

PATTERNS—

Lettering:
Enlarge 140%

Ribbon & Bells:
Enlarge 125%

Lettering:
Enlarge 140%

Stars:
Enlarge 125%

SANTA ON SKATES
WOODWORKING INSTRUCTIONS—

TOOLS & SUCH

Plywood, $3/8$" x 12" x 12"
Plywood, $1/4$" x 13" x 4"
Scroll saw
Tracing paper
#2 lead pencil
Graphite paper
Paper towels
Sandpaper, medium-grit and
　fine-grit
Tack cloth
Wood glue
Sawtooth picture hanger

CUT IT OUT

1 With tracing paper, duplicate the patterns. Turn the tracing over and rub over the pattern lines with a #2 lead pencil. You may transfer the design with a commercial graphite paper, but you'll want to eliminate messy excess graphite by wiping over the graphite with a paper towel. Transfer the patterns onto the wood. Cut the plaque from $3/8$" plywood. Cut the banner from $1/4$" plywood.

GET IT SANDED

1 Before assembly, make sure that all parts are finish sanded, with their sharp edges "killed" or slightly rounded, and that all tool marks are removed. Use a medium-grit sandpaper to sand the saw-cut pieces. Switch to a fine-grit sandpaper and sand again. Then lightly wipe over all surfaces with a tack cloth to pick up the dust created by sanding. (Don't firmly rub the tack cloth over the wood—the cloth will leave an unwanted tacky residue.)

PUT IT TOGETHER

1 You can now begin painting. When painting is finished, glue the banner to the plaque, using the broken line for placement. Then, paint the back. Install the sawtooth picture hanger at the center top of the back of the plaque—not the banner.

SANTA ON SKATES
PAINTING INSTRUCTIONS—

STUFF YOU GOTTA HAVE

Pure Pigment Paint Colors
  Ivory Black
  Titanium White
Acrylic Paint Colors
  Brown Sugar (medium brown)
  Christmas Red (bright red)
  Coastal Blue (sky blue)
  Dove Gray (light gray)
  Evergreen (medium green)
  School Bus Yellow (deep yellow)
  Victorian Rose (light skintone)
Clear acrylic spray
Brown paper bag or old cotton rag
Ruler
#2 lead pencil
White graphite paper
Paper towels
Round brush, #4 or #5
Flat brush
Liner brush
Stylus

DO IT LIKE THIS

1 After you've prepared the wood, paint the banner front Evergreen. Then, paint the edges Ivory Black. Leave the back unpainted for now. Let the paint dry. Use a piece of brown paper bag or an old cotton rag to smooth the painted surfaces. Wipe off the sanding dust. (Acrylic paint often raises the grain of the wood.)

2 Transfer the lettering onto the banner with white graphite paper. Paint the lettering Titanium White. Add all remaining banner details with Ivory Black.

3 Transfer the patterns for the border, the sky, the snow, and the lake onto the plaque with white graphite paper. Notice the broken line indicating the position where the banner is to be placed. Do not paint above this broken line. Do not transfer Santa or the snowflake dots yet.

4 Paint the sky Ivory Black. Mix Titanium White and Coastal Blue, 3:1, and fill in the lake. Let the paint dry. Paint the left snowy hill Titanium White. While the paint is wet, working quickly, dab in small amounts of Coastal Blue to shade the top of the hill. Use a slightly wet flat brush to pull streaks of the wet Titanium White from the hill down onto the lake. (With this technique, you achieve the look of snow reflecting in the icy lake.) Paint the right hill in the same manner.

5 Measure in $\frac{1}{2}$" from the outer edges of the plaque front and draw a crooked pencil line. Use your pencil to draw the checks along the border. Make certain you have enough checks to alternate colors completely around the board. (Don't attempt to make the checks perfectly matched in width. Part of the charm of folk art is the lack of conformity in shapes and style.)

6 Base-coat all checks School Bus Yellow, then paint the Christmas Red checks. Let the paint dry. Use a piece of brown paper bag or an old cotton rag to smooth the painted surfaces. Wipe off the sanding dust.

7 Transfer the Santa outline onto the plaque with white graphite paper. Fill in the entire shape with Titanium White. Copy the details onto the Santa. Paint Santa's coat, hat, and pants Christmas Red. Fill in his face with Victorian Rose. Mix Titanium White and Christmas Red, 3:1, and lightly blush the cheeks and fill in the bottom lip. Paint Santa's belt Ivory Black with a School Bus Yellow buckle. Add School Bus Yellow coat buttons and paint the coat belt loops Christmas Red. Fill in the boots and the mitten with Evergreen. Paint the skate straps Brown Sugar and the skate blades Dove Gray. Fill in all fur trim, his beard, and his mustache with Titanium White.

8 Fill in the trees on the hillsides with Evergreen. Using the large end of a stylus, dip into Titanium White and dot the snowflakes. Using the small end of a stylus, dip into Titanium White and dot the belt hole dots. With a liner brush, add the Titanium White lines above and below the hat pom-pom. Let the paint dry. Using a liner brush, add all of the outlining, Santa's facial features, and any remaining details with Ivory Black. Let the paint dry.

9 After you've glued the banner to the plaque, paint the back of the banner and the back of the plaque Ivory Black. Use a piece of brown paper bag or an old cotton rag to smooth the painted surfaces. Wipe off the sanding dust. Apply clear acrylic spray to all wood surfaces. Finally, install the sawtooth picture hanger.

SANTA ON SKATES
PATTERNS—

Banner:
Enlarge 125%

Santa Plaque:
Enlarge 145%

HOLIDAY HEARTS
WOODWORKING INSTRUCTIONS—

TOOLS & SUCH

For each ornament:
Pine, 1/4" x 9" x 9"
Scroll saw
Tracing paper
#2 lead pencil
Graphite paper
Paper towels
Drill
Drill bit, 1/8"
Sandpaper, medium-grit and
   fine-grit
Tack cloth
5-minute epoxy

CUT IT OUT

1 With tracing paper, duplicate the patterns. Turn the tracing over and rub over the pattern lines with a #2 lead pencil. You may transfer the design with a commercial graphite paper, but you'll want to eliminate messy excess graphite by wiping over the graphite with a paper towel. Transfer the patterns onto the wood. Cut the star and heart from 1/4" pine. Drill a 1/8" hole in the star for hanging.

GET IT SANDED

1 Before assembly, make sure that all parts are finish sanded, with their sharp edges "killed" or slightly rounded, and that all tool marks are removed. Use a medium-grit sandpaper to sand the saw-cut pieces. Switch to a fine-grit sandpaper and sand again. Then lightly wipe over all surfaces with a tack cloth to pick up the dust created by sanding. (Don't firmly rub the tack cloth over the wood—the cloth will leave an unwanted tacky residue.)

PUT IT TOGETHER

1 You can now begin painting. When painting is finished, glue the heart to the star. Finally, using the raffia, hang the ornament.

HOLIDAY HEARTS
PAINTING INSTRUCTIONS—

STUFF YOU GOTTA HAVE

Pure Pigment Paint Colors
   Napthol Crimson
Acrylic Paint Colors
   Old Ivy (deep green)
   School Bus Yellow (deep yellow)
Antiquing Medium
   Apple Butter Brown
Brown paper bag or old cotton rag
#2 lead pencil
White graphite paper
Paper towels
Flat brush
Woodburner, optional
Brass plumber's brush, optional
Tack cloth, optional
Sandpaper, fine-grit
5-minute epoxy
Raffia

DO IT LIKE THIS

1 After you've cut and sanded the wood, transfer the checks onto the heart with white graphite paper. Use a woodburner to burn all penciled border lines. If you've never used a woodburner, here are some important things to remember: Set the tip down and pull it toward you, following the pattern lines. For even lines, keep the tool moving at an even pace. To remove carbon buildup on the tip, use a brass plumber's brush. Use tack cloth to wipe away the woodburned particles.

If you prefer, paint the checks without burning the lines.

2 Paint the checks, alternating Old Ivy and Napthol Crimson. Apply the Napthol Crimson to the edge of the heart. Leave the back of the heart unpainted. Paint the star front and edges School Bus Yellow. Leave an unpainted area in the center of the star where the heart attaches. (You'll get a much better bond with the glue if you glue raw wood to raw wood.) Let the paint dry. Use a piece of brown paper bag or an old cotton rag to smooth the painted surfaces. Wipe off the sanding dust. (Acrylic paint often raises the grain of the wood.)

3 Antique the heart and star fronts and edges with Apple Butter Brown antiquing medium, avoiding the unpainted star center. Let the antiquing dry. To give a primitive, aged look, sand the painted surface of the star with a fine-grit sandpaper to remove some of the paint. Wipe off the sanding dust.

4 Using 5-minute epoxy, attach the heart to the star. Then, paint the ornament back with the color of your choice. Finally, using the raffia, hang the ornament.

HOLIDAY HEARTS

PATTERNS—

Heart:
Reproduce 100%

Star:
Reproduce 100%

PAINT DIRECTORY

FOLKART PAINT COLORS BY NUMBER—

Pure Pigment Paint Colors
- Burnt Sienna 568
- Cerulean Blue Hue 562
- Cobalt Blue 561
- Dioxazine Purple 558
- Ivory Black 576
- Napthol Crimson 555
- Phthalo Green 563
- Pure Orange 553
- Red Light 554
- Sap Green 565
- Titanium White 574
- Ultramarine Blue 560
- Yellow Medium 552
- Yellow Ochre 572

Acrylic Paint Colors
- Almond Parfait 705
- Barnyard Red 611
- Berries 'n Cream 752
- Bluebell 909
- Blue Ribbon 719
- Brown Sugar 707
- Buckskin Brown 418
- Buttercrunch 737
- Cherry Royale 758
- Christmas Red 958
- Clover 923
- Coastal Blue 713
- Cotton Candy 929
- Country Twill 602
- Dove Gray 708
- Earthenware 610
- Evergreen 724
- Georgia Peach 615
- Green 408

- Harvest Gold 917
- Heartland Blue 608
- Magenta 412
- Maple Syrup 945
- Molasses 943
- Old Ivy 927
- Persimmon 919
- Plantation Green 604
- Potpourri Rose 624
- Primrose 930
- Promenade 912
- Rusty Nail 914
- School Bus Yellow 736
- Shamrock 926
- Strawberry Parfait 751
- Sunset Orange 746
- Sweetheart Pink 955
- Taffy 902
- Tapioca 903
- Thunder Blue 609
- Ultramarine 720
- Victorian Rose 620
- Wicker White 901

Antiquing Medium
- Apple Butter Brown 820

Other brand name products
used on projects in this book:
- Krylon 1303 clear acrylic spray
- Deft wood sealer
- Sanford Sharpie ultra-fine point
- Pilot gold marker extra-fine point

METRIC CONVERSIONS

INCHES TO MILLIMETRES AND CENTIMETRES

MM-Millimetres   CM-Centimetres

INCHES	MM	CM	INCHES	CM	INCHES	CM
$1/8$	3	0.9	9	22.9	30	76.2
$1/4$	6	0.6	10	25.4	31	78.7
$3/8$	10	1.0	11	27.9	32	81.3
$1/2$	13	1.3	12	30.5	33	83.8
$5/8$	16	1.6	13	33.0	34	86.4
$3/4$	19	1.9	14	35.6	35	88.9
$7/8$	22	2.2	15	38.1	36	91.4
1	25	2.5	16	40.6	37	94.0
$1^{1}/_{4}$	32	3.2	17	43.2	38	96.5
$1^{1}/_{2}$	38	3.8	18	45.7	39	99.1
$1^{3}/_{4}$	44	4.4	19	48.3	40	101.6
2	51	5.1	20	50.8	41	104.1
$2^{1}/_{2}$	64	6.4	21	53.3	42	106.7
3	76	7.6	22	55.9	43	109.2
$3^{1}/_{2}$	89	8.9	23	58.4	44	111.8
4	102	10.2	24	61.0	45	114.3
$4^{1}/_{2}$	114	11.4	25	63.5	46	116.8
5	127	12.7	26	66.0	47	119.4
6	152	15.2	27	68.6	48	121.9
7	178	17.8	28	71.1	49	124.5
8	203	20.3	29	73.7	50	127.0

YARDS TO METRES

YARDS	METRES	YARDS	METRES	YARDS	METRES	YARDS	METRES	YARDS	METRES
$1/8$	0.11	$2^{1}/_{8}$	1.94	$4^{1}/_{8}$	3.77	$6^{1}/_{8}$	5.60	$8^{1}/_{8}$	7.43
$1/4$	0.23	$2^{1}/_{4}$	2.06	$4^{1}/_{4}$	3.89	$6^{1}/_{4}$	5.72	$8^{1}/_{4}$	7.54
$3/8$	0.34	$2^{3}/_{8}$	2.17	$4^{3}/_{8}$	4.00	$6^{3}/_{8}$	5.83	$8^{3}/_{8}$	7.66
$1/2$	0.46	$2^{1}/_{2}$	2.29	$4^{1}/_{2}$	4.11	$6^{1}/_{2}$	5.94	$8^{1}/_{2}$	7.77
$5/8$	0.57	$2^{5}/_{8}$	2.40	$4^{5}/_{8}$	4.23	$6^{5}/_{8}$	6.06	$8^{5}/_{8}$	7.89
$3/4$	0.69	$2^{3}/_{4}$	2.51	$4^{3}/_{4}$	4.34	$6^{3}/_{4}$	6.17	$8^{3}/_{4}$	8.00
$7/8$	0.80	$2^{7}/_{8}$	2.63	$4^{7}/_{8}$	4.46	$6^{7}/_{8}$	6.29	$8^{7}/_{8}$	8.12
1	0.91	3	2.74	5	4.57	7	6.40	9	8.23
$1^{1}/_{8}$	1.03	$3^{1}/_{8}$	2.86	$5^{1}/_{8}$	4.69	$7^{1}/_{8}$	6.52	$9^{1}/_{8}$	8.34
$1^{1}/_{4}$	1.14	$3^{1}/_{4}$	2.97	$5^{1}/_{4}$	4.80	$7^{1}/_{4}$	6.63	$9^{1}/_{4}$	8.46
$1^{3}/_{8}$	1.26	$3^{3}/_{8}$	3.09	$5^{3}/_{8}$	4.91	$7^{3}/_{8}$	6.74	$9^{3}/_{8}$	8.57
$1^{1}/_{2}$	1.37	$3^{1}/_{2}$	3.20	$5^{1}/_{2}$	5.03	$7^{1}/_{2}$	6.86	$9^{1}/_{2}$	8.69
$1^{5}/_{8}$	1.49	$3^{5}/_{8}$	3.31	$5^{5}/_{8}$	5.14	$7^{5}/_{8}$	6.97	$9^{5}/_{8}$	8.80
$1^{3}/_{4}$	1.60	$3^{3}/_{4}$	3.43	$5^{3}/_{4}$	5.26	$7^{3}/_{4}$	7.09	$9^{3}/_{4}$	8.92
$1^{7}/_{8}$	1.71	$3^{7}/_{8}$	3.54	$5^{7}/_{8}$	5.37	$7^{7}/_{8}$	7.20	$9^{7}/_{8}$	9.03
2	1.83	4	3.66	6	5.49	8	7.32	10	9.14

INDEX